Box Office

18
WHO DOES HOLLYWOOD SAY THAT I AM?

Youth will learn how filmmakers view the Savior through several distinctly different films: *Jesus of Nazareth*, *The Gospel According to Matthew*, *Jesus*, and *Godspell*.

42
THE HEAVENLY RETREAT

The collection of films in this retreat — *City of Angels*, *Ghost*, *Always*, *Heaven*, and *Defending Your Life*—offer different glimpses into heaven. Film, study, and discussion help youth form an understanding of heaven and the afterlife.

54
THE HUNCHBACK OF NOTRE DAME

Youth find sanctuary in this retreat that explores how Christ turns lives topsy-turvy and how he desires every day to be a festival of kindness to all our neighbors.

60
A RACISM RETREAT

"Red and yellow, Drak, and white. . . ." *Drak?!* Racism, bigotry, and prejudice pose enormous barriers between individuals and groups of people. Based on *Enemy Mine*, *A Family Thing*, and *To Kill a Mockingbird*, this race retreat shows different types of discrimination and the amazing grace that enables us to overcome these divisions.

70
SPORTS MOVIE MARATHON

Kick off a knockout sports-filled retreat for fathers and sons. Using the movies *Hoosiers*, *Rocky*, and *Rudy*, it scores with youth by dealing with hope, faith, and love.

77
THE PREACHER FEATURE

Youth get to explore the nature of ministry; and through the characters in *The Apostle* and *Leap of Faith*, they'll view different types of ministers—flaws and all.

82
MULAN

Mulan discovers that her own courage and determination are personal traits, not necessarily inherent gender traits. God likewise calls us to what we are to be through love and grace.

88
A FANTASTIC RETREAT

The animated features *Antz* and *A Bug's Life* serve as catalysts for exploring how to confidently respond to God's call to leadership.

Innocence Lost

A Retreat With Sessions Based On *Pleasantville, Dave,* and *Big.*

PURPOSE Youth will explore the nature of innocence—how we lose it and how it can be returned to us through the grace of Jesus Christ.

THEME We are all born with a certain level of innocence; but eventually we fall victim to temptation, sin, selfishness, and evil. Only in God's love and grace through Jesus Christ can we return to a place where we are seen as innocent in the eyes of God.

USING THESE SESSIONS & ACTIVITIES

This retreat is designed around one, two, or all three of the films being shown in their entirety. Using a one-session format would require a lengthy time slot or viewing the film(s) at an earlier time. Review key scenes, if necessary, during activities that emphasize those scenes. If you only have time for clips, be prepared to provide an account of the missing story parts to maintain the narrative continuity. Please note the cautions for each film and preview each one in its entirety. Send home a Student Movie Pass (parent consent form on the inside back cover) if necessary.

MATERIALS
- Videos: *Pleasantville, Dave,* and *Big*
- TV and VCR
- Bibles
- Chalkboard, dry erase markerboard, or flip chart with markers
- Index cards
- Masking tape; small candies such as lollipops, M&Ms®, Hershey Kisses®, cinnamon Jolly Ranchers®, or other "hot" candy for use as prizes

WHAT IS INNOCENCE?
Ask the youth what they think innocence or being innocent means. After the discussion, point out any of the following definitions not mentioned, being sure to note the difference between innocence and naiveté. If you wish, list the definitions in advance on a large sheet of paper or a chalkboard (keep covered at first).

- Freedom from sin, evil, or guilt (Adam and Eve's state before they ate from the tree of the knowledge of good and evil)
- Freedom from the knowledge of evil
- Purity (doing or thinking nothing that is morally wrong or impure)
- Freedom from the harmful, corrupting effects of evil
- Naturally trusting or childlike
- Not likely to harm, injure, or corrupt another person
- Not likely to deceive or manipulate other people
- Not guilty of a specific crime or offense (as in a jury verdict of "Not Guilty")

WHAT IS NAIVETÉ?

Naiveté carries with it the following connotations:

- A lack of worldly wisdom (a simplistic outlook)
- A lack of sophistication (as in a lack of experience)
- A refusal to see the world realistically (being unaffected by experience or unwilling to learn from it)
- A refusal to acknowledge the possibly manipulative intentions of those around you (an insistence on seeing all people as "good")

Leave all the definitions posted in plain sight throughout all the sessions. They will be the foundation for the discussions of specific characters in the films.

First Things First

At the beginning of each movie discussion, ask the following group of questions, customizing them to fit each film. Then proceed with the additional questions listed under each session. Always feel free to modify any of the items or to add others.

Using the various definitions of innocence from the opening session, guide the youth in exploring how _____ (the town of Pleasantville, Dave, or Josh from *Big*) exhibited innocence (for instance: How were they free from sin, evil, or guilt? How were they free from the knowledge of evil? How did they demonstrate purity? and so on through all the definitions). Encourage the youth to give examples from all the characters in each movie. Do the same with the definitions of naiveté.

VIDEO VIEWING
To reference key scenes in *Pleasantville*, use the Video Viewing chart below.

Suggestion: Preview the film on the VCR that you will use with the program. Make note of these key scenes so you can fast forward during the program, using these approximate start times and your VCR counter.

Start	Event	Count
0:02	Depressing facts about living in the nineties	_____
0:09	TV repairman appears	_____
0:13	Transported into the TV	_____
0:26	Mr. Johnson just keeps wiping.	_____
0:31	Lover's Lane	_____
0:36	Skip sees one red rose.	_____
0:41	"It never changes. It never gets any better or any worse."	_____
0:49	"I baked them for you."	_____
0:51	"What's outside of Pleasantville?"	_____
0:57	Mom becomes colorized; Bud helps her cover it with makeup.	_____
1:00	Art book: "Where am I going to see colors like that?"	_____
1:07	Mr. Johnson washes off Betty's gray.	_____
1:11	Apple: garden of Eden	_____
1:13	Dad comes home; Mom's not there. He's lost.	_____
1:16	Meeting at the bowling alley; real rain falls.	_____
1:24	Prejudice against "the coloreds"	_____
1:27	"You don't deserve paradise!"	_____
1:28	David defends his "sitcom" mom.	_____
1:33	Second town meeting	_____
1:37	"I don't know what I would do if I couldn't paint."	_____
1:41	The trial	_____
1:48	Goodbyes: Jennifer goes to college; David returns home.	_____
1:53	David realizes how much his real mom needs him.	_____

SESSION 1:
Pleasantville

· ·

The woman said to the serpent, "We may eat of the fruit of the trees in the garden; but God said, 'You shall not eat of the fruit of the tree that is in the middle of the garden, nor shall you touch it, or you shall die.' " But the serpent said to the woman, "You will not die; for God knows that when you eat of it your eyes will be opened, and you will be like God, knowing good and evil." So when the woman saw that the tree was good for food, and that it was a delight to the eyes, and that the tree was to be desired to make one wise, she took of its fruit and ate; and she also gave some to her husband, who was with her, and he ate. Then the eyes of both were opened, and they knew that they were naked.
Genesis 3:2-7

Question 3: Did the people of Pleasantville have the knowledge of good and evil before David and Jennifer arrived on the scene? What happens after the townspeople have the knowledge of good and evil? (Possible examples of evil: prejudice, hatred, suffering, violence, intolerance, and mob mentality. Possible examples of good: Mr. Johnson discovers his talent for art, the mother begins to make a life for herself, the father learns how to express his love, David learns to be assertive, Jennifer goes to college, and so forth.)

Question 4: Do you know persons who exhibit the qualities of innocence? Do you know anyone you would call naive? (Avoid using specific names.)

BACKGROUND
Pleasantville is 124 minutes long and is rated PG-13.

CAUTIONS
Pleasantville is rated PG-13 primarily because it presents some mature sexual themes. There are a few slips in language, implied sexual relationships, and a discussion between the sitcom mom and her daughter that leads to her discovering her own sexuality.

SYNOPSIS
A '90s brother and sister are magically transported into the "rerun" world of a '50s family sitcom. In the process of adjusting to their new environment and attempting to get back home, they introduce free will into the deterministic sitcom world with chaotic results. They learn significant lessons about themselves that change their lives forever.

DISCUSSING & LEARNING
Read aloud Genesis 3:2-7, then ask these questions:

Question 1: [Refer to the recommended opening discussion outlined in "First Things First" on page 2. Customize the question to fit *Pleasantville*.]

Question 2: How is *Pleasantville* like the garden of Eden or a paradise? (Possible answers: no crime, the basketball team never loses, you can eat all you want and never get fat, everybody looks good, no pain, no homelessness, no prejudice, and so on. Note the scene in which the TV repairman says, "You don't deserve paradise.")

SESSION 2:

Dave

. . . .

For it is God who is at work in you, enabling you both to will and to work for his good pleasure. Do all things without murmuring and arguing, so that you may be blameless and innocent, children of God without blemish in the midst of a crooked and perverse generation, in which you shine like stars in the world.

Philippians 2:13-15

BACKGROUND
Dave is 110 minutes long and is rated PG-13.

CAUTIONS
Dave is rated PG-13 primarily because it presents some adult sexual situations. There are a few slips in language, and there is an adulterous sexual relationship between the real President Mitchell and one of his secretaries during which he has a stroke.

SYNOPSIS

Dave is the small-town owner of an employment agency, who bears an uncanny resemblance to the US President. When Dave is asked to double for the President at an upcoming event, he sees it as the adventure of a lifetime. When the President has a stroke, his conniving Chief of Staff arranges for Dave to continue posing as the President until he can maneuver himself into higher office. Dave brings joy and fun to the White House but must eventually accept responsibility for the corrupt actions of the real President.

DISCUSSING & LEARNING

Read aloud Philippians 2:13-15 and ask the following questions:

Question 1: [Refer to the recommended opening discussion outlined in "First Things First" on page 2. Customize the question to fit *Dave.*]

Question 2: How does Dave first approach the idea of standing in as the real President? (At first he is afraid, but then he sees it as a great adventure—a way to have fun. He believes he is doing good).

Question 3: When does Dave begin to understand the consequences of what he is doing? (when the homeless shelters are vetoed, and later, when he realizes how President Mitchell was involved in the savings-and-loan scandal)

Question 4: Everyone says the Vice President is a "good man." Why do you think they say this about him? Is Dave a good man? (personal opinion)

Question 5: Why do you think Duane would have been willing "to take a bullet" for Dave? (personal opinion)

Question 6: Read Philippians 2:13-15 again, then ask this question: How do you think Dave shines like a star "in the midst of a crooked and perverse generation"? (Dave's decision to take responsibility for the real President Mitchell's actions accomplishes the greatest good for the greatest number of people).

VIDEO VIEWING
To reference these key scenes in *Dave*, use the Video Viewing chart below.

Start	Event	Count
0:05	The real President Mitchell's "nasty side"	_____
0:10	Dave doubles for the President.	_____
0:20	The conspiracy unfolds.	_____
0:35	The First Lady	_____
0:37	Dave as the compassionate president	_____
0:43	"Would you take a bullet for me?"	_____
0:46	The homeless shelter	_____
0:53	Finding the money for the shelters with Murray's help	_____
0:56	The budget-cutting cabinet meeting	_____
1:03	The first lady discovers the truth.	_____
1:18	Dave fires Bob Alexander.	_____
1:20	The Jobs Program press conference	_____
1:25	Meeting with the Vice President	_____
1:31	Heart to heart with the Vice President	_____
1:34	Dave admits his guilt before a joint session of Congress.	_____
1:41	"I would've taken a bullet for you."	_____

SESSION 3:
Big

. . . .

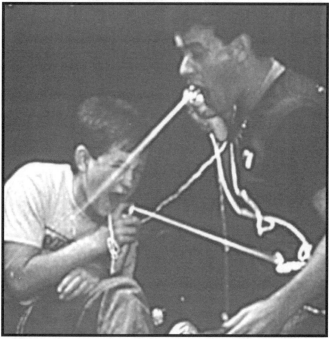

Let no one despise your youth, but set the believers an example in speech and conduct, in love, in faith, in purity.

1 Timothy 4:12

You who were once estranged and hostile in mind, doing evil deeds, he has now reconciled in his fleshly body through death, so as to present you holy and blameless and irreproachable before him.

Colossians 1:21-22

BACKGROUND
Big is 104 minutes long and is rated PG.

CAUTIONS
Big is rated PG primarily because it presents some adult sexual situations. There are a few minor slips in language and sexual relationships are implied.

SYNOPSIS
When twelve-year-old Josh Baskin wishes to become "big" while using a fortune-telling machine at a local carnival, he wakes up the next morning to find that his wish has been granted. He is then forced to deal with adult realities as a twelve-year-old in a man's body until he can find a way to reverse the process.

DISCUSSING & LEARNING
Question 1: [Refer to the recommended opening discussion outlined in "First Things First" on page 2. Customize the question to fit *Big*.]

INNOCENCE LOST AND INNOCENCE REGAINED
Read aloud 1 Timothy 4:12 and ask the following questions:

Question 2: Why does Josh wish to be "big"?

Question 3: In what ways does Josh's innocence help him as an adult? In what ways does it hurt him?

Question 4: What would be the first thing you would do if you suddenly became an adult? (personal opinion)

Read aloud Colossians 1:21-22 and ask the following questions:

Question 5: Josh tells Susan that there are "a million reasons for going home" but only one for staying. What do you think some of Josh's reasons for going home were? (personal opinion)

Question 6: What do you think are some of the lessons Josh learned from being an adult? Point out the relationship between Josh's experience and our experience as Christians. When we fall victim to temptation, sin, selfishness, and evil, God gives us the option of asking for forgiveness and accepting God's grace through Jesus Christ.

THE POWER OF GOD'S GRACE
Read aloud the Scripture once more, this time reading Colossians 1:19-23. Ask the following questions:

Question 7: How do we experience God's grace? (through Jesus' death on the cross and the power of his resurrection)

Question 8: What do we gain by accepting God's grace? (We become "holy and blameless and irreproachable before [God]." In God's eyes we are "innocent" by all the definitions we have listed here.)

Question 9: What is required of us after we accept God's grace? (to "continue securely established and steadfast in the faith, without shifting from the hope promised by the gospel that you heard")

INNOCENCE LOST MUSICAL CHAIRS

Give each youth seven index cards. Have the participants create "Experience Cards" by writing each of the following items on separate cards: First Kiss, First Date, First Time Falling in Love, First Time Driving Alone, First Broken Heart, First Job, and First Time Away From Home. Have each youth hold on to his or her cards as you play music of their choice for musical chairs. As with regular musical chairs, there is one less chair than the number of persons playing. When the music stops, one person will be left without a chair. In this version of the game, however, the person left without a chair must give up one of his or her "Experience Cards." Play until someone has given up all his or her "Experience Cards."

NOW BE HONEST! ACTIVITY

Lay down a masking tape starting line at one end of your meeting room (the line should be long enough for the whole group to stand on it side by side.) Make sure everyone can walk forward unobstructed. Have the participants stand on the starting line side by side. The leader announces, "I have a series of statements here, and I want you to take one step forward for each statement that is true for you—Now Be Honest!"

1. Found out about Santa Claus before age 12.
2. Found out about Santa Claus before age 8.
3. Found out about Santa Claus before age 6.
4. Cheated on a test at school and got caught.
5. Cheated on a test at school without getting caught.
6. Told a white lie to keep from getting in trouble.
7. Skipped school.
8. Sneaked out of the house without your parents knowing about it.
9. Stole something from a store and got caught.

VIDEO VIEWING
To reference these key scenes in *Big*, use the Video Viewing chart below.

Start	Event	Count
Opening Sequence	Josh as a little boy	_____
0:06	The trip to the carnival	_____
0:10	The fortune-telling machine	_____
0:12	Josh wakes up "big."	_____
0:20	Josh and Billy go to New York.	_____
0:23	Josh is afraid to spend the night alone.	_____
0:30	Josh starts work.	_____
0:36	Josh's first paycheck	_____
0:38	Josh meets the boss at FAO Schwartz.	_____
0:40	The "Heart and Soul" piano dance	_____
0:42	Josh is promoted.	_____
0:44	Product testing meeting	_____
0:48	Josh's apartment	_____
0:50	The party	_____
0:59	Trampoline: Josh teaches Susan the power of play.	_____
1:07	"What's so special about Baskin?" "He's a grown-up!"	_____
1:09	Josh starts to ignore Billy.	_____
1:14	First kiss	_____
1:16	Josh begins acting more like an adult.	_____
1:22	The confrontation with Billy	_____
1:24	Josh gets homesick and visits his neighborhood.	_____
1:26	Josh tells Susan.	_____

Big Trivia:

Big was originally supposed to be directed by Steven Spielberg, who intended to cast Harrison Ford as Josh Baskin.

10. Stole something from a store and did not get caught.
11. Had a party at your house when your parents were gone.
12. Got someone in trouble on purpose.

OPTIONAL LEARNING ACTIVITY

Look for *The Diaries* [or Diary] *of Adam and Eve* by Mark Twain, which contains "Eve's Diary" and "Extracts From Adam's Diary." (Another possible title is *The Private Life of Adam and Eve.*) Go to a public library or any comprehensive collection of Mark Twain's works. These diaries are about the garden of Eden as told from Eve's and Adam's points of view. Twain provides a new perspective on the story of humankind's loss of innocence. "Eve's Diary" is especially touching in that it was written less than a year after Twain's wife, Livy, passed away. You could read it to the youth at a "storytime" or have the youth read selected excerpts to one another.

13. Sneaked into a movie without paying.
14. Lied about your age to get into the movie for the child's price.
15. Lied about your age to impress someone.
16. Carried a fake ID.
17. Figured out who the Tooth Fairy is without the help of friends.
18. Climbed over a locked fence.
19. "Borrowed" money out of your parent's purse or wallet without asking.
20. Lied to your parents about spending the night with a friend and then going somewhere else.

After the last statement, the leader tells everyone to freeze. The leader then surveys the room and says that the third of the group still close to the starting line is the "Babes in the Woods" crew; their theme song is "Baby Face" (or some other innocent-sounding tune), which they must sing in order to receive a lollipop. The group close to the middle is now known as "Semi-Sweet"; they have to sing "I Don't Wanna Grow Up!" to get their prizes—chocolate kisses. Finally, the third group, those farthest from the start line, are all "Born to Be Wild!" and, of course, have to sing that song to get their cinnamon Jolly Ranchers® (or some other "hot" candy). (If the youth don't know one or more of the songs, have them make up words and a tune.) Hand out the candy and ask everyone to sit together in the middle of the floor for further discussion.

What Do These Three Movies Have in Common?

At first it might seem that *Pleasantville*, *Dave*, and *Big* do not have much in common. After you have watched these films, however, you will see that they share a common theme: the loss of innocence. All three screenplays were written by Gary Ross, who also directed *Pleasantville*.

FORREST GUMP
GUMP CAMP, THE RETREAT

For everything there is a season, and a time for every purpose under heaven.

**Ecclesiastes 3:1,
New Revised Standard Version**

The entire Scripture (Ecclesiastes 3:1-8) goes with the song "Turn, Turn" on the *Forrest Gump* soundtrack.

THEME Forrest Gump asked simple questions and made simple yet truthful observations about the complexities of life. Likewise, Jesus Christ calls us to live the simple ideal of treating our neighbors as precious children of God.

PURPOSE Youth will focus on the moments Forrest was Christlike to his neighbors. The youth will be challenged to look for opportunities in which they can be Christlike for their neighbors as well.

© 1994 BY PARAMOUNT PICTURES. PHOTO BY PHIL CARUSO.

GUMP CAMP ACTIVITIES

A retreat-full of Gump Camp activities are described here and on the next two pages.

GUMPARDY! Test the knowledge of the youth group's biggest Gump know-it-alls. Answers and questions are on page 14.

TOUCH FOOTBALL Weather permitting, hold the Shrimp Bowl of touch football. For a touchdown to count, the scoring team must shout, "Stop, Forrest, Stop!" And remember the team prayer.

ELVIS IMPERSONATION CONTEST Crank up music by the King and hold a competition for the best—or worst—impersonation. Thankyaverymuch.

BACKGROUND
Forrest Gump is 142 minutes long and is rated PG-13.

CAUTIONS
The movie contains profanity, premarital sex, a trip to a strip bar, hints of parental sexual abuse, and realistic war scenes. If you play the soundtrack during breaks, you may want to be selective about some of the songs. One lyric includes the line, "Everybody must get stoned." The movie is representative of changes that have occurred in American history. Please preview the entire film before you use this program and send home a Student Movie Pass (parent consent form on the inside back cover) if you think that it is necessary.

SYNOPSIS
Tom Hanks inspires viewers through his portrayal of "Forrest, Forrest Gump." The movie spans three decades of American history. Special effects put Forrest right in the middle of the action. He even gets to meet three Presidents. Forrest

© 1994 BY PARAMOUNT PICTURES. PHOTO BY PHIL CARUSO.

rises from a child with a disability to a football star, from a Vietnam hero to a multimillionaire. He can be seen as a Christ figure throughout the movie. Forrest may not have been a smart man, but he knew what love was.

MATERIALS
- *Forrest Gump* video—for viewing and possibly as a prize for Gumpardy! (page 14)
- VCR and TV
- Nametags
- *Forrest Gump* soundtrack (play during breaks)—This could also be used as a prize for "Life Is Like" Contest.
- Paper and markers for "Life Is Like" Contest
- Elvis music for the Elvis Impersonation Contest and Elvis T-shirts to use as prizes—one shirt for middle school and one for high school
- Table tennis table, balls, and paddles for the tournament. Don't forget a sign-up sheet for participants.
- Copies of Life Questions for small groups (page 13
- A box of chocolates to spring on the group during Discussing & Learning
- Forrest Gump-like food. Possibilities are popcorn shrimp; "Run, Forrest, Run" cake; Dr. Peppers® (also for the Dr. Pepper® Drinking Contest); cookout stuff; soft drinks and cookies for break times; popcorn for the movie; and the like. Good sources for Gump recipes are *Bubba Gump Shrimp Co. Cookbook: Recipes and Reflections from Forrest Gump* (ISBN 0-8487-1479-2) and *Forrest Gump: My Favorite Chocolate Recipes* (ISBN 0-8487-1487-3).
- For an in-town retreat, host families might provide breakfasts; but involve the youth in KP duty as a service and in helping with meals.
- Rooming list—Check with the retreat center; some require this list in advance.
- Football and different-color shirts or flags that will help members identify their team for the Shrimp Bowl

BEFORE THE SESSION
Recruit adult helpers. Try to recruit one adult for every eight youth. Give these helpers specific instructions (or written guidelines). You may want to have a meeting prior to the retreat to discuss guidelines and expectations and to help ease volunteers' anxieties.

Room setup is essential! Some games require movable sturdy chairs, and others require lots of room. Decide where small groups will meet.

LIFE IS LIKE CONTEST
The winner is the person who best completes the sentence "Life is like. . . ." (Just as Forrest said, "Life is like a box of chocolates. You never know what you are going to get.") Ask: "Why do you say that?" It might be helpful to come up with a few possibilities beforehand in case the group needs a starter. Discuss the humor and seriousness of each answer.

LIFE QUESTIONS FROM FORREST GUMP
Form small groups consisting of no more than eight youth and a leader. Have each person draw a slip of paper with a question from the Life Questions on page 13 and discuss each question within the small group. After this session, collect each group's questions and reuse them at another small-group session later in the retreat.

THINGS TO REMEMBER WHEN ORGANIZING A RETREAT

- Set a registration deadline (3–4 weeks prior to the event). Count on last-minute add-ons and dropouts. Always check the refund policies of the retreat center or hotel. If you are hosting an in-town retreat, prepare to have an extra house available to host youth in case a family emergency cancels a house already committed.

- When staying in a hotel, make sure that you check all rooms in advance for damage. Report damage to the front desk to save your damage deposit when you check out. When hosting an in-town retreat, make sure that the host families understand their responsibilities; give them guidelines for the retreat.

- Make sure that there is plenty of food. If the retreat is a theme event such as "Gump Camp," be creative. For instance, a cake with the words "Run, Forrest, Run" on it is a great touch.

- Always leave retreat facilities cleaner than you found them. If you do, you will be warmly received when you visit again.

DISCUSSING & LEARNING

Join in an opening prayer: "Almighty God, remind us that you created each and every one of us in your image. And your image is diverse, complex, and interesting. We celebrate the differences in each of us, which make us your unique children. Thank you for life and life abundant. In Jesus Christ we pray. Amen."

Use the following narrative to create your own youth talk. (You may want a youth to lead the session.)

Retard, loser, freak, gimp, stranger, redneck, Charlie, druggie, alcoholic, cripple, stupid, different, stripper, baby killer, sinner. What is normal? And who gets to decide?

"Life is like a box of chocolates." Variety is all around us, but we rarely look for the beauty in one another. Much of our time is spent trying to cut others down. We try to neatly categorize one another. We fail to see God's magnificent work in ourselves and in others.

Forrest was called many names. However, he (like Jesus during his trial and crucifixion) never retaliated. Instead, Forrest always looked for the best in others. When the boys on the bus told Forrest that there was no room, he didn't yell at them. He simply kept looking for his place.

Answer these questions aloud or to yourselves:
- Whom do you know or see daily who acts like Forrest?

- How do you view this person? Describe him or her.
- How do you suppose God views this person?

Forrest saw Jenny as the beautiful love of his life. He was deeply committed to her although she seemed ungrateful.

Answer these questions aloud or to yourselves:
- Whom do you know who acts like Jenny?
- How do you view this person? Describe him or her.
- How do you suppose God views this person?

Forrest couldn't understand why people made such a big deal about African Americans wanting to go to

DR. PEPPER® DRINKING CONTEST
Line 'em up and knock 'em back. The winner of the 30-second contest might win a six-pack of Dr. Pepper®. Gee, thanks a lot!

TABLE TENNIS TOURNAMENT
Post sign-up sheets, make brackets, and paddle away! Give the winner a fast-food gift certificate or some other clever prize.

POPCORN SHRIMP FEAST
Don't limit the soiree to popcorn shrimp. You can try your boiled shrimp, your barbecued shrimp, your shrimp kabob, or any other concoction you and your youth come up with. See Forrest Gump cookbook suggestions under Materials on page 10.

© 1994 BY PARAMOUNT PICTURES. PHOTO BY PHIL CARUSO.

Answer these questions aloud or to yourselves:
- Whom do you know who has felt like Lt. Dan?
- How do you view this person? Describe him or her.
- How do you suppose God views this person?

When Forrest got rich, he shared his money with Bubba's mother; and even she asked him if he was crazy. Jesus himself had been referred to as "God's own fool." Forrest was classified a fool by the educational system. Jesus gave all he had to help others. Forrest risked his life to save his friends in the war. Jesus forgave those who killed him. Forrest continually forgave Jenny, who took advantage of his love.

Too often, we play the part of Jenny. We take advantage of God's love and grace. We do our own thing and look for love elsewhere. We are ungrateful, but God still loves us. Too often, we give up on others. We end relationships instead of trying to reconcile. We judge others as unworthy of our time and love. We do not forgive, and we do not forget.

Forrest offered chocolate to people he did not know, to people who did not want any, even to people who thought he was crazy. [Pass a box of chocolates around the group, if you have one.] God offers love to us even when we do not think we need it and when we do not deserve it. Was Forrest a real person? No, but the world sure needs people like him.

school with whites at the University of Alabama. Instead of spitting on the black girl as she entered the building for her first day of class, he (a football star) helped her by returning a book she had dropped. Forrest grew to love Bubba, a black fellow soldier, who had an especially large lip and talked endlessly.

Answer these questions aloud or to yourselves:
- Whom do you know or see daily who acts like Forrest?

- How do you view this person? Describe him or her.
- How do you suppose God views this person?

Forrest saved several of his fellow soldiers, including Lt. Dan Taylor. Lt. Dan was unappreciative. Forrest had to remind him that even without legs he was still Lt. Dan Taylor.

Watch the movie again. Look for times when Forrest does something Jesus might have done. Then pay close attention to your everyday life. Look for ways you can be Christlike to those with whom you come in contact. The world sure needs you.

Photocopy the following questions. Then cut the copied questions apart into strips. Have the members of small groups draw a question and read it to the group. Ask the group members to respond.

- Forrest's mom said, "Don't let anyone tell you they are better than you." Who do you compare yourself with? Why? What happens when you feel that you do not measure up?

- What does *normal* mean?

- Forrest's mom slept with the principal to get Forrest into school. Why do you think she did that? How far do you think you would go to help someone you love a lot? What boundaries do you have for yourself in getting what you want?

- "God didn't make us all the same," Forrest's mom said. Why do you think we are so drawn to conformity?

- On Forrest's first day to ride the bus, he met Dorothy Harris. After introducing himself, he said, "We ain't strangers no more." Did you ever meet a stranger and become instant friends with him or her? Why, do you think, was he or she so easy to like?

- Jenny once prayed to become a bird to escape from her dad. What do you pray for most? Have you ever prayed to escape from someone or a certain situation? What did you do after praying?

- "A promise is a promise." How do you feel when you discover that someone has been dishonest with you? How hard is it to keep your promises?

- Forrest began to run amazingly fast while he was being chased. It was a miracle, according to his doctor. Have you ever had a miracle happen to you? If so, describe your miracle.

- When Forrest got on the bus for school, several people said, "Seat's taken!" Have you ever felt like there was no place for you? Describe the feeling and how you handle those times.

- Jenny and Forrest were "like peas and carrots." Who is your best friend and why?

- "Sometimes we do things that don't make sense." What do you do when life does not make sense? Who helps you deal with the inconsistencies?

- If shoes tell a lot about a person, what story would the pair you are wearing right now tell? Would they tell where you've been? where you're going? Describe the happiest time in your life since owning your current pair of shoes. Describe the worst time. What would you like to see happen in your future?

- Do you ever wish you had said something to a friend or done something for a friend that you did not say or do?

- Forrest's mom told him that his dad was on vacation when he possibly had left them. Is it OK for parents to lie? In what circumstances might a lie be OK? How does this affect a Christian, when honesty is to be highly valued?

- One day Forrest and Jenny returned to the house where she grew up. She began to throw rocks at the house as she remembered her growing-up years. What do you think Forrest meant when he said, "Sometimes there just aren't enough rocks"? How would you rate your growing-up years on a scale of 1 to 10, with 10 being perfect? Why did you pick that number? If you could change one thing in your life history, what would you change?

- Forrest cut the local school football field grass for free. What job would you do for free?

- What do you think Forrest's mother meant when she said, "Life is like a box of chocolates"?

- What is the best gift you have ever received?

- Bubba had a big lip. Have you ever chosen not to be friends with someone because of the way he or she looked? Why do you think our society puts so much emphasis on physical appearance?

- Whom would you miss the most if you moved away or were gone tomorrow?

- Forrest rescued Jenny from the nudie bar and Lt. Dan from the jungle. Neither was thankful. Have you ever helped someone only to find her or him ungrateful? Do you ever get tired of helping people?

- What similarities can you find between Forrest and Jesus?

- What expectations do you have to live up to? Who puts the most pressure on you?

- What scares you the most?

- What do you think your destiny is?

- Jenny told Forrest she had a virus (possibly AIDS) that doctors could not cure. He married her anyway because he loved her. Could you have done that?

- When Forrest got rich, he gave Bubba's mother Bubba's share. Would you have done this? Why or why not?

- Jenny asked Forrest what he wanted to be; and he responded, "Ain't I gonna be me?" What does it mean to be you?

- Forrest could run like the wind. Tell the group about one of your talents.

- Jenny once asked Forrest to pray with her. Do you have a friend with whom you can pray? How do you feel when someone tells you that he or she is praying for you?

GUMPARDY!
ANSWERS & QUESTIONS

Use these questions to see who remembers the most about the movie. Play a game similar to Jeopardy!® with three youth who feel that they are Gump gurus. Have them write down their answers and reveal them to the group. Give the winner a prize such as a box of chocolates or a copy of the movie. Remind the youth that their response must be in the form of a question.

A The last name of Forrest's friend Jenny.
Q What is Curran?

A The full name of Forrest's friend Bubba.
Q What is Benjamin Buford Blue?

A Two things you can tell about a person by his or her shoes.
Q What is, "where they have been and where they are going"?

A Forrest and Jenny were like these tasty vegetables.
Q What are peas and carrots?

A The US Army, including Forrest's troops, looked for Vietnamese soldiers they referred to by this common name.
Q Who is "Charlie"?

A Rain fell for this number of months while Forrest was in Vietnam.
Q What is four?

A The college football legend who coached Forrest at the University of Alabama.
Q Who is Paul "Bear" Bryant?

A The uniform number that Forrest wore at Alabama.
Q What is 44?

A The US Army rank, held by Forrest, that is abbreviated PFC.
Q What is Private First Class?

A The Tennessee city where Jenny made her singing debut.
Q What is Memphis?

A Lt. Dan's last name.
Q What is Taylor?

A Forrest needed to catch this bus to get to Jenny's home in Montgomery.
Q What is Number 9?

A The bus driver who drove Forrest to school.
Q Who is Dorothy Harris?

A You'll wear these in your hair if you are going to San Francisco.
Q What are flowers?

A Lt. Dan's fiancée.
Q Who is Susan?

A It's how long Forrest ran in years, months, days, and hours.
Q What is 3 years, 2 months, 14 days, and 16 hours?

A Forrest could eat this many chocolates . . . or so he said.
Q What is 1½ million?

A A derogatory term for a person with a physical disability, it was Forrest's boyhood nickname.
Q What is "Gimp"?

A Greenbow County High School shared this mascot with a Major League baseball team in the South.
Q What are the Braves?

A The cause of the deadly disease that Jenny contracted.
Q What is an unknown virus, possibly HIV/AIDS?

A The date Jenny died.
Q What is March 22, 1982?

A The blonde actress whose picture was in President Kennedy's bathroom.
Q Who is Marilyn Monroe?

WEEKEND YOUTH RETREAT

Then the ones who pleased the Lord will ask, "When did we give you something to eat or drink? When did we welcome you as a stranger or give you clothes to wear or visit you while you were sick or in jail?" The king will answer, "Whenever you did it for any of my people, no matter how unimportant they seemed, you did it for me."

Matthew 25:37-40

Jesus asked a second time, "Simon son of John, do you love me?" Peter answered, "Yes, Lord, you know I love you!" "Then take care of my sheep," Jesus told him.

John 21:16

"You've been reduced to nothingness. You have no money, no job, no car, no home, no family to speak of. Life itself has beaten you to a bloody pulp. You're as dependent on the Transition Home's help as a child is on its mother."

Former Homeless Resident
Transition Home for Women in Crisis
Open Door Community House
Columbus, Georgia

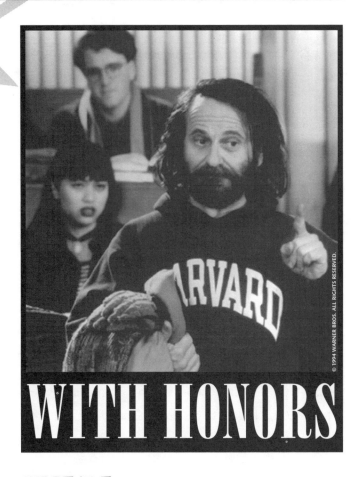

WITH HONORS

THEME Christ calls us to reach poor and homeless people in our community.

PURPOSE Youth will increase their awareness of homelessness and consider the Christian response to this issue. Youth involved in this retreat will examine opportunities for service.

VIDEO VIEWING

To reference these key scenes in *With Honors*, use the Video Viewing chart below.

Suggestion: Preview the film on the VCR that you will use with the program. Make note of these key scenes so you can fast forward during the program, using these approximate start-end times and your VCR counter.

Start-End	Event	Count
0:00–0:02	Opening narrative: You must "crush others" to succeed.	_____
0:10–0:13	Monty finds Simon in the library basement, burning Monty's thesis. Simon says, "You want something; I need something."	_____
0:13–0:14	Monty describes the man holding his thesis hostage as a worthless, stinking, filthy, useless human being.	_____
0:17–0:18	Simon accuses Monty of not thinking of him as human at all.	_____
0:18–0:19	Monty offers Simon the van to live in.	_____
0:25–0:26	Monty takes Simon a blanket.	_____
0:26–0:28	Simon offers to carry Monty's books.	_____
0:29–0:32	Two pages for a bath. Roommate overreacts to the presence of Simon, spouts off stereotypical remarks about the homeless.	_____
0:32–0:34	Interview with social worker.	_____
0:36–0:38	Simon tells about his life.	_____
0:41–0:47	Simon attends class with Monty.	_____
0:47–0:51	Monty tries to get roommates to let Simon stay in basement when it goes below freezing.	_____
0:57–1:00	Message from Simon via a friend.	_____
1:00–1:02	Monty tracks down Simon on the street.	_____
1:02–1:04	Monty takes Simon in; Simon agrees to go on disability.	_____
1:11–1:13	Simon gets last roommate to accept him as a person.	_____
1:24–1:30	Monty sacrifices graduating with honors, and all four friends take Simon to see his son.	_____

BACKGROUND

With Honors (1994) is 101 minutes long and is rated PG-13.

CAUTIONS

With Honors contains profanity, implied sexual encounters, and a "morning after" shot with brief nudity. Preview the entire film before the retreat. Please send home the Student Movie Pass (parent consent form on the inside back cover) if you think that it is necessary.

MATERIALS

- *With Honors* video
- Any videos listed on bottom portion of these retreat pages that you feel are appropriate for your group
- VCR and TV
- Nametags
- Photocopies of Facts/Myths About Homelessness (page 21)
- Large boxes: refrigerator, washing machine, clothes dryer, or other large cardboard boxes—two per small group—broken down (flattened); duct tape; plastic bags; newspapers; milk jugs; empty jars; twine
- Four pads of large poster paper, four markers, four Bibles
- Different colors of large plastic cups for youth and group leaders
- "Food stamps" (rolls of coupons, tickets, receipt books)
- Literature from agencies that serve the homeless in your area

HOMELESSNESS PORTRAYED ON FILM

Most recent movies that offer an accurate portrayal of homelessness generally include more questionable material—usually language, violence, or nudity—than can be used as a central part of a homeless retreat. Several movies, though not suitable for viewing in their entirety by most youth groups, do have meaningful segments that would enrich the homelessness retreat experience. Here are some:

God Bless the Child (1988), 93 minutes, NR (made for TV), World Video Enterprises, Inc., now available from Gospel Films

The best, and certainly the most harrowing, film about homeless persons. Offering no easy or happy solutions, this is the story of a young mother (Mare Winningham) working as a hotel maid. When her building is condemned, she and her daughter are put on the street. She loses her job because of difficulties in finding care for her daughter. The story follows them through a series of demeaning experiences in shelters

SYNOPSIS AND OVERVIEW FOR LEADERS

Youth involvement with the poor begins with education and interaction. In *With Honors,* college student Monty risks what is most important to him, graduating with honors, due to a committed friendship with Simon, a homeless man. The film shows that personal contact can break down barriers and prejudice between people. Monty and Simon find extraordinary acceptance of each other when each does something for the other out of kindness rather

Matt Dillon and Danny Glover portray two homeless men trying to make their lives better in *Saint of Fort Washington.*

The Homeless Covenant

This weekend, we will be in solidarity with the poor and homeless in our community. We covenant to eat or drink only what is provided by the Soup Kitchen. We will not eat or drink anything from other sources. We will not change clothes or bathe until after dinner on Saturday night. We will completely refrain from using luxuries such as make-up, boom boxes, and video games.

than as part of their "deal." The ensuing friendship affects others, including Monty's roommates and Simon's estranged family. In *With Honors,* Simon is as much Monty's redeemer as Monty is Simon's.

Christ charges us, as disciples, to care for one another and those in need. His call is specific. We are to care not only for those we love, but also for those we do not love and do not know.

Factors contributing to the nationwide homeless rate are very complex. Misconceptions about homelessness add to public hesitancy in supporting shelters and agencies. Welfare reform places a greater burden on those agencies and relief organizations.

USING THESE SESSIONS & ACTIVITIES

The Homeless Retreat is designed to be a structured, systematic weekend for youth. WEEKEND AT THE MOVIES recommends the following itinerary for the retreat, including specified days and times for activities and often-strict do's and don'ts. The purpose for the rigid structure is that it best reflects the lives of homeless people. This format will

and the social services system, until at last the mother must make a heart-rending decision concerning the welfare of her daughter.

While not widely available earlier, *God Bless the Child* may now be ordered from Gospel Communications. If you choose to do so, view the film during the weekend. Order the film for $14.95

plus shipping and handling from Gospel Communications, 800-253-0413. Every church member, young and old, should see this powerful, heart-wrenching film.

The Saint of Fort Washington
(1993), 104 minutes, Rated R, Warner Home Video
With two incredibly powerful performances by Danny Glover and

Matt Dillon, this is the story of the friendship that develops between two homeless men—and the possibility that one of them might be a saint. The title refers to the huge shelter for homeless men in New York City, which can be as dangerous as the streets it is supposed to protect them from. The R rating is due to street language and a violent death at the end of

RETREAT SCHEDULE
Friday Evening

Arrive, check in, make room assignments, settle in, and have dinner together in the Soup Kitchen.

Orientation: Prior to dinner, gather outside the Soup Kitchen. Read the quotation from the former Transition Home resident, and announce the Homeless Covenant for the retreat.

Have a leader ask a blessing before entering the Soup Kitchen for the evening meal. Take a 30-minute break after dinner and chores.

increase individual awareness of homelessness and poverty in your community. Emphasis should be on understanding and compassion. Awareness will lay the groundwork for future involvement. Leaders should familiarize themselves with local agencies, shelters, and outreach programs that use youth volunteers. Be prepared to direct interested youth to service within one week of the retreat.

Also, youth group members may come to the retreat with personal stories in which they set out to help others but received much more than was given. Encourage this witness and point out that redeemers are found in unlikely places. Each member of the group is a potential agent of grace, through a kind word, a selfless gesture, volunteer efforts, outreach projects through the church, and many other ways.

BEFORE THE RETREAT

Successful activities in the retreat require ample space and movable, sturdy chairs. Decide on locations for all activities ahead of time. Call the church dining hall the Soup Kitchen and issue "food stamps" to "purchase" meals and snacks. Establish a comfortable theater area to view the film. Distribute boxes of crackers and a jar of peanut butter rather than individually wrapped cracker snacks. Take leftover food to a local food pantry or shelter after the retreat.

Scenes from suggested films at the bottom of these pages make good filler for free time between sessions and activities. Please preview these films before showing them to youth. Homelessness has been portrayed in the movies, but generally the scenes are graphic.

Friday, 7:30 PM

Theater

SESSION 1: AFTER-DINNER MOVIE AND DISCUSSION

- Have popcorn and drinks available.
- Ask the youth and the leaders not to discuss the film until breakout groups are established after the show.
- Serve drinks in different-color cups. Alternate the colors so that the kids can sit with their friends during the movie but will be separated into a group by their cup color afterward.
- After viewing *With Honors*, groups adjourn to talk about the film, the Homeless Covenant (see page 17), and the theme for the weekend.

the film. Near the beginning, however, is a great illustrative scene of Dillon suffering the confusion, indifference, and dehumanization of our huge welfare bureaucracy—and in which there's a minimum of offensive language.

The Fisher King (1991), 138 minutes, Rated R, Columbia TriStar Home Video

This fascinating retelling of the legend of the *Quest for the Holy Grail* is set in the midst of New York's urban decay and human derelicts. About an hour into the film, there is a scene in Grand Central Station in which a crippled beggar, a Vietnam veteran, sets forth a quirky philosophy of beggars and donors. The R rating is due to strong street language and violence. This scene

involves profane language, so leaders should view it critically before deciding to use it.

Hero (1992), 116 minutes, Rated R, Columbia TriStar Home Video
Self-centered conniver and convicted thief Bernie LaPlant (Dustin Hoffman) saves a plane load of passengers when their plane crashes near his car. LaPlant tells the homeless John

SMALL GROUP ACTIVITY

Say: "Make a list of 10 places to go if you had no home." Encourage everyone to offer ideas and to put them in order of best to worst places (example: #1 a relative's house—#10 doorway on the street). Allow 15–20 minutes to make lists. Then convene in the theater, keeping each group together. Take turns allowing each group to read aloud their #1, #5, and #10 options.

Ask if anyone knows persons who have had to resort to these options. Review Simon's options in *With Honors*. Close with a prayer of thanksgiving for our homes, safe places to go, and for the continued work of those who provide safe places for homeless people. Tell everyone to meet in the theater *before* breakfast for a few minutes in the morning. Adjourn, reminding everyone: "Food and drinks are available only from the Soup Kitchen."

Saturday, 7:30 AM

Before anyone eats or drinks, convene in the theater. Engage the youth in casual conversation as they come in; enlist the adult volunteers and small group leaders to help.

Eventually the youth will announce that they are hungry. Ask the group to settle down and read the Scripture passages for the weekend retreat, noting these key themes: "Lord, when were you hungry and I gave you something to eat?" and "If you love me, then feed my sheep."

Close with the following prayer or a similar blessing before going into the Soup Kitchen for breakfast: "Lord, bless this food to our use and us to thy service. Please, God of mercy, make us mindful of the needs of others." Use this blessing before every meal, asking the group to learn it and say it in unison.

Saturday, 10:00–11:00 AM

Theater

SESSION 2: PERSONAL RESPONSE TO THE HOMELESS

THEME God accepts each of us unconditionally, whether we are poor or rich, clean or dirty, hungry or full.

Meet in the theater and review scenes from *With Honors*. Break into small groups. Each group needs a Bible, paper, and a marker. Each group should designate a reader, a writer, a person sympathetic toward the homeless, and a person antagonistic toward the homeless. Have each group look up passages that describe the poor in society. Use a concordance or slips of paper with verses that you have chosen beforehand. Within each group the reader will read the passage aloud and the writer will record what the group thinks is the key theme or message.

DISCUSSING & LEARNING

Question 1: How do you feel when you see homeless people?

Question 2: What do you do when confronted by homeless people?

Question 3: What caused each of Monty's roommates to accept Simon Wilder as a human being?

Think up scenarios involving street people. Ask the group antagonist to respond to the situation and then the sympathetic person to respond. Roleplaying can be useful for this exercise—have the antagonist act as a homeless person and ask the sympathetic person for money or food or a job. Then swap roles and see what comments are made from the actors and from the group.

Question 4: What are some positive responses to homeless people? List the responses.

CLOSING

Close with a prayer that we respond to the poor and homeless in our community in a positive way and that God will help us love the unlovable.

Distribute plastic bags and announce that there will be a 45-minute break before lunch. Tell the youth that while they are on break, they are to find items to decorate a cardboard house they will be constructing during the afternoon session. Instruct them to bring to lunch everything they found during the break.

Bubber, who gives him a lift in his car, what he has done. When the TV station, whose star reporter (Geena Davis) was among the rescued, offers a million-dollar reward, Bubber comes forward with the proof that Bernie has given him—one muddy shoe to match the one he lost at the rescue site. Bubber begins to use the money for good causes, including aid for homeless persons. Halfway through the film, there is a poignant scene: Bubber has eaten a fine meal in a fancy restaurant, while outside several homeless persons pass by, sometimes pausing to look in. When a young person asks Bubber for his autograph, he agrees provided that the other person goes out and helps the homeless. An otherwise delightful twist on the Cinderella story and a satire on our media age, which offers up packaged heroes, the film is marred by excessive profanity, including the "F-word."

Curly Sue (1991), 102 minutes, Rated PG, Warner Home Video
A bit syrupy, in that it's the kind of formula film of which Shirley Temple made so many, this tale of a homeless waif and her adoptive dad could be used with a junior high

Saturday, 12:00 PM

Lunch in the Soup Kitchen

Have everyone line up outside the closed doors of the Soup Kitchen just before lunch for the blessing. Free time is until Session 3. Remind the youth to collect items from around the church to use in the next session and that food and drinks are available only from the Soup Kitchen.

Saturday, 1:30–3:00 PM

Large Classroom Setting

SESSION 3: HOW DO THE HOMELESS SURVIVE?

Before the session, remove all but a few chairs from the room. Pile the cardboard boxes in the center of the floor. Have newspapers, jars, duct tape, plastic bags, and other "trash" in piles around the room. As the youth arrive, ask them to find their group leader. Explain that this is an exercise in street survival, and point out that statistics show it is often safer to live on the street than in a shelter.

Each small group will make a cardboard house. A few youth may take advantage of the chairs left in the room. Draw an analogy between the uncomfortable situation that exists with the youth having few places to sit, and being homeless, with nowhere to sit or rest.

Before dispersing to find cardboard and other shelter materials, some may want to grab chairs for their group's house. Ask each person to guard the articles collected during the breaks. Sometimes people steal possessions left in the open. During construction, ask each group to discuss problems of homelessness.

After one hour of construction, have show and tell. Ask someone from each group to describe the problems of shelter and how they solved them. Then ask everyone to form a circle and close with the prayer that those in real need find shelter. (Depending on the weather and other safety-related conditions, some youth may wish to sleep outside in their shelters.)

Call free time until dinner, reminding everyone that food and drinks are available only from the Soup Kitchen.

Saturday, 5:30 PM

Dinner in the Soup Kitchen

Line up outside the closed doors of the Soup Kitchen for a blessing before dinner. After dinner, allow 30 minutes free time after chores.

Saturday, 7:30 PM

Large Classroom Setting

SESSION 4: FACTS ABOUT HOMELESSNESS

After everyone has arrived, ask if anyone has bathed or changed. Open with a prayer.

Distribute copies of "Facts/Myths About Homelessness" (page 21) to pairs of youth. Have pairs read it and discuss any surprising information. Then call on a few persons to tell one fact or myth that surprised them.

Break into the small groups. Each group needs paper and a marker. Tell the groups the following facts:

- To move from homelessness to independent living, a person must save about $1,200 for housing and utility deposits.
- In most states, if a family becomes homeless and the children are in the custody of the state, parents cannot get their children back until they can provide housing in which each child has a room, or in which no more than two children of the same gender share a room.
- To apply for a job, a person must have a permanent address and phone number.
- Homeless persons sometimes hold down three or four jobs in fast-food and other service areas.
- Hopelessness is the most common feeling among the homeless.
- For every month a woman has been in a crisis situation, it usually takes one month to get out. Average recovery times range from six months to three years.

Have each group discuss and list the essentials for setting up housekeeping (housing and utility deposits; apartment or house payments; accounts for gas, electricity, phone, water, sewer, garbage pick-up, and others). Make another list of ways

group. Curly Sue (Alison Porter) and her guardian (James Belushi) have been surviving mainly by taking advantage of gullible, well-off people. But when they try their scam on a lawyer obsessed with her career (Kelly Lynch), they get more than they bargained for.

Home Alone 2, Lost in New York (1992), 120 minutes, Rated PG, Fox Video
This rather lame-brained knock-off of the first *Home Alone* film has an interesting character who appears about mid-film and then at the end. You could show the first scene and ask the group what kind of person she is as a test of stereotyping. Because of her unkempt appearance

and strange actions, most people will say that she's a homeless person. The movie never says that she is. We shall call her "The Pigeon Lady," who might just be an eccentric living a lifestyle others would call weird.

to provide for the resources needed to set up housekeeping (stay in school, get a good education, find a job, budget money well, live within means, save enough to live on for three months if unemployed).

Bring the groups back together. Have someone from each group tell two things from the group's list of essentials. Have another person tell two things from the how-to list.

CLOSING
Close with a prayer for continued understanding about the realities of homelessness. Announce free time until lights out. Remind everyone that food and drinks are available only from the Soup Kitchen.

Sunday, 8:30 AM
Breakfast in the Soup Kitchen

Have everyone line up outside the closed doors of the Soup Kitchen for a blessing. Arrange a display of literature from agencies that serve the homeless in your area. Have sign-up sheets on the tables for youth to add their names to the mailing lists of these agencies.

Sunday, 9:30 AM
Vesper Service in the Auditorium or Large Classroom

Use these Scripture passages—John 21:15-17 and Matthew 25:37-40—as responsive readings. Then ask the participants to share feelings and insights about the weekend.

Invite the youth to suggest things the group can do to serve the poor and homeless after the retreat. (Call attention to the literature or other information from the various service agencies and programs for the homeless in your area.) Include Holy Communion in the service, if possible; or close with a charge, read in unison, to accept and help the homeless.

FACTS / MYTHS ABOUT HOMELESSNESS

Fact: The basic cause of homelessness in the US is the inability of poor people to afford housing.

Myth: Most homeless people are mentally ill. (The national average is 23 percent with the homeless population averaging 33 percent, which includes serious depression as a mental illness.)

Fact: The chance of a woman being molested in a shelter is 14 percent. The chance of any shelter resident being robbed is 49 percent. Contagious diseases, such as the drug-resistant strain of tuberculosis, are more hazardous now than they have been for decades.

Fact: Due to their limited resources, the poor face impossible choices between food, shelter, daycare, basic needs, utilities, and clothing.

Myth: Almost all of the homeless are alcoholics or drug users. (Only about 33 percent of the homeless are substance abusers.)

Fact: Substance abuse increases the risk of displacement for the precariously housed, but getting one's drug or alcohol problem under control is not necessarily a ticket off the street.

Fact: According to the National Alliance to End Homelessness, on any given night 750,000 Americans will be without shelter. Between 1.3 million and 2 million Americans will be homeless at some time during the year.

Myth: Most of the homeless are lazy misfits. (In some areas, working people make up 30 percent or more of the homeless population.)

Fact: Families with children represent about 35 percent of the homeless population and are the fastest growing subgroup among the homeless.

Fact: Women who are homeless usually end up that way because of domestic violence. Single women make up 12 percent of the homeless, and women with children make up 34 percent.

Myth: More mentally ill persons are now homeless because of "deinstitutionalization." (This phenomenon occurred prior to 1975; the dramatic increase in the number of homeless in this country has occurred since 1980.)

Fact: The large increase in homelessness did not occur until the 1980's when incomes and housing options for those living on the fringes began to diminish rapidly.

Sleepy Movie Sleepover

In the days when the judges ruled, there was a famine in the land, and a certain man of Bethlehem in Judah went to live in the country of Moab, he and his wife and two sons. The name of the man was Elimelech and the name of his wife Naomi, and the names of his two sons were Mahlon and Chilion; they were Ephrathites from Bethlehem in Judah. They went into the country of Moab and remained there. But Elimelech, the husband of Naomi, died, and she was left with her two sons. These took Moabite wives; the name of one was Orpah and the name of the other Ruth. When they had lived there about ten years, both Mahlon and Chilion also died, so that the woman was left without her two sons and her husband.

Ruth 1:1-5

In the sixth month the angel Gabriel was sent by God to a town in Galilee called Nazareth, to a virgin engaged to a man whose name was Joseph, of the house of David. The virgin's name was Mary. And he came to her and said, "Greetings, favored one! The Lord is with you." But she was much perplexed by his words and pondered what sort of greeting this might be. The angel said to her, "Do not be afraid, Mary, for you have found favor with God. And now, you will conceive in your womb and bear a son, and you will name him Jesus. He will be great, and will be called the Son of the Most High, and the Lord God will give to him the throne of his ancestor David. He will reign over the house of Jacob forever, and of his kingdom there will be no end." Mary said to the angel, "How can this be, since I am a virgin?"

Luke 1:26-34

GRACEFUL RELATIONSHIPS

All three movies feature characters who encounter unexpected situations and who must change their plans accordingly. In *Sleepless in Seattle*, happily married Sam doesn't expect to lose his wife to cancer. Similarly, Annie doesn't expect to question her devotion to her fiancé, based on a voice she hears on a radio talk show. In *While You Were Sleeping*, Lucy's boring, predictable life is turned upside down when a subway customer is mugged and she leaps in front of a moving train to rescue him. Of course, no one at Aurora's birthday party expects the beautiful princess of Disney's *Sleeping Beauty* to fall victim to an evil woman's curse.

Both of the Scriptures feature Bible characters whose lives were altered because of unexpected circumstances. Naomi, an Israelite woman living in a foreign land, suddenly found herself without a husband or sons at a time when women without men were often at the mercy of merciless people. Mary, probably only fourteen or fifteen years old, discovered that she was unmarried and pregnant, a situation that usually brought shame and punishment.

What do all of these situations have in common? In every case, the characters found grace in the situation and acted accordingly. We usually think of grace in the God-human context. In that relationship, God freely gives love that we do not deserve and can never earn. That love frees us from sinful lives because we are changed from the inside out. In other words, when we encounter this marvelous love, our natural reaction is to live lives that reflect God's love for us. But there is another context for grace, and that is in human to human relationships. When we imitate God by giving love freely, without strings attached, both we and the recipients of that love are changed.

A person who offers grace to someone often sees something that the someone could not see in herself or himself. Grace provides a new vision of who we are because someone who cares about us understands and accepts us. We are then liberated to let others know who we really are and not worry about what others think. In grace-filled relationships there is no judgment, just love. When we are involved in grace-filled relationships, we are free to be what God created us to be. If we both provide grace and seek others who will offer it to us, we can more easily cope with life's unexpected turns.

THEME Life doesn't always turn out the way we plan it. Because of this, we can best achieve happiness by seeing the grace in any situation and by living our lives as reflections of that grace.

PURPOSE This retreat will increase mother-daughter communication about relationship issues.

MATERIALS
- *Sleepless in Seattle, While You Were Sleeping,* and Disney's *Sleeping Beauty* videos
- TV and VCR
- Food and dining supplies
- Index cards, pencils, bulletin board, pushpins or tacks, paper, envelopes, paper bag, several pieces of poster paper, masking tape, world map (optional)

Participants should bring
- Items for an overnight stay

USING THE RETREAT AND ACTIVITIES

This sleepover retreat is ideally used as a mother-daughter weekend retreat, designed to begin with Friday night dinner and end after Saturday night dinner. It can be adapted to shorter or longer settings. Remember when inviting participants, chances are that not all the girls in your youth group live with their birth mothers. Some girls may prefer to invite a stepmother, older sister, or other important woman in their life. Discuss the matter privately with anyone you think might need special consideration.

mirror, mirror, on the wall

SESSION 1: SIS (*SLEEPLESS IN SEATTLE*)

BACKGROUND

Sleepless in Seattle (1993) is 105 minutes long and is rated PG.

CAUTIONS

This film contains mild swearing and brief verbal references to premarital sex. An engaged couple is shown in the same bed, but no sexual language or actions occur.

SYNOPSIS

Widower Sam Baldwin mourns his beloved wife so deeply that his anxious son, Jonah, calls a nationwide radio talk show to ask for advice. Reluctantly, Sam tells his story on the air; and thousands of women send him letters offering companionship. One listener is Annie Reed, whose letter appeals most to Jonah. But Sam isn't interested in blind dates, and Annie is engaged. What follows is a combination of luck and destiny, and the two *MFEO* (made for each other) lovers finally meet and fall in love despite seemingly overwhelming obstacles.

SECRET LETTER MESSAGES

As participants gather for Friday's meal, hand each a card with block letters that represent familiar expressions. Some examples from the video include *MFEO* (made for each other), *H and G* (hi and goodbye), *YOH* (your only hope). Other suggestions are *H and K* (hugs and kisses), *DTD* (do the dishes), *YDU* (you don't understand), *PUYR* (pick up your room), *CIP* (crisis in progress), *CIL* (crazy in love). Add others that may be familiar to your group. Tell participants that they should try to figure out what the letters stand for and write their guesses on the backs of the cards. The group will discuss their answers later.

OPENING PRAYER

Pray: "Lord, we gather in this place seeking to learn more about the kind of love you offer us all. Teach us to love one another the way you love us. Amen."

INTRODUCE THE THEME AND THE VIDEO

After dinner, read or paraphrase "Graceful Relationships," page 23.

Answer questions and allow discussion until you feel that everyone has a better understanding of God-human and human-human grace. Watch *Sleepless in Seattle* in one sitting.

SECRET LETTER MESSAGES, CONTINUED

After the movie, ask everyone to tell his or her guesses on the lettered cards that were handed out at dinner. There are no wrong answers as long as the guesses match the letters. Tell the participants that a stack of cards and some pencils will be placed on a table. When anyone thinks of a message that can be reduced to a few letters, she is to write the letters (with the answer written on the back) and post the card on a centrally located bulletin board. As others pass by during the retreat, they can write their guesses on the front of the cards. Before leaving Saturday evening, everyone can reveal the answers. This activity is bound to produce some lasting *SLM*s (secret letter messages) that will bond the group in the weeks and months ahead and remind them of the retreat.

TELL STORIES OF HOW YOU MET SOMEONE SPECIAL

The next activity is a great group-builder. Say: "Sam and Annie didn't meet until the last scene. Can you remember how you met someone you care about? Don't say anything yet. Take a piece of paper and write about how you met your husband, boyfriend, best friend, or some other special person in your life. Don't mention names. When you finish, place the story in an envelope and place it in the paper bag. When everyone is done, we will mix the envelopes up and each person will read aloud someone else's story. Then we'll all try to guess whose story it is."

DISCUSS GRACE

Question 1: Remember that offering grace to persons means seeing them for who they really are and loving them just as they are. Most people will respond to such non-judgmental love by trying to be the person God created him or her to be. Did you find any grace-filled relationships in *Sleepless in Seattle*?

Answer 1: Jonah and Sam love each other unconditionally. Although there are occasional conflicts, both seem motivated by true love for each other. Annie's relationship with her friend Becky is another example. When Annie seems to be acting irresponsibly in her relationship with Walter, Becky keeps loving Annie for who she is. Even Walter exhibits grace when Annie breaks up with him. He seems to care most deeply about her happiness and the honesty of their relationship.

Question 2: Suppose you decide that you want to fill your life with as many grace-filled relationships as possible. Which relationships would be the most important ones to concentrate on?

Answer 2: Answers will vary. Some will say mother-daughter, man-woman, or friend-friend relationships.

Question 3: What would be some ways that a romantic relationship could be based on grace?

Answer 3: Answers will vary. Some characteristics might include non-judgmental, honest, patient, empathetic.

SESSION 2: ON THE RIGHT TRACKS

BACKGROUND

While You Were Sleeping (1995) is 103 minutes long and is rated PG.

CAUTIONS

This film contains minor swearing and some references to human anatomy set in a humorous context.

SYNOPSIS

Lucy's job collecting tokens for the transit authority leaves her plenty of time to dream about romance and far-off destinations. But in reality, her only company is her cat; and her life is going nowhere. She fantasizes about a handsome stranger, who comes through her toll station every day; but she can't work up the courage to introduce herself to him. Fate takes a hand when the stranger, Peter Callahan, is mugged and she saves his life. While Peter lies in a coma in the hospital, Peter's family mistakenly believes that Lucy is his fiancé. His family practically adopts Lucy, and she can't bring herself to disappoint them by telling them the truth. Worse yet, she falls in love with Peter's brother, Jack. By the time the happy ending arrives, Lucy has learned the value of love and truth.

MORNING DEVOTIONS

Ask someone to read the Scriptures, then lead the following discussion:

Question 1: What do these Scriptures have in common?

Answer 1: Some may answer that the central characters are women, which is true. The answer to look for, however, is that both Naomi and Mary found themselves in unexpected circumstances that could have proved disastrous.

Question 2: Despite the fact that life didn't turn out the way they had planned it, both Naomi and Mary were involved in grace-filled relationships that helped them face adversity successfully. Do any of you know these Bible stories well enough to tell us who helped these women?

Answer 2: Naomi's daughter-in-law Ruth gave her the kind of love God gives us—totally devoted and full of sacrifice. Ruth left her homeland to follow Naomi, and she never left Naomi's side. (Optional: Read the brief Book of Ruth from the Bible to hear this beautiful story.) Mary's fiancé, Joseph, could have shamed and rejected her; but he married her and provided a good home for Jesus and his siblings.

Ask everyone to watch for examples of grace while watching *While You Were Sleeping*. When the youth think that they see an example of grace, they should point it out immediately. Pause the VCR and discuss the reasons why they think grace is evident in the scene. Some examples are noted with their approximate location (hour:minute) below:

0:26–0:29 Peter's family makes orphan Lucy feel like one of them, despite the fact that they know practically nothing about her.

0:45–0:46 Lucy's reaction to Jack's rocking chair frees him to trust in his own talent and ability instead of simply taking over his father's established business.

1:13–1:16 Jack's father gives him the freedom to follow his own dream.

1:32–1:36 Lucy tells the family that their love has liberated her to become a fiancé (a French word that comes from a Latin word that means "to trust"), a daughter, a granddaughter, a sister, and a friend.

GIVE EACH OTHER THE WORLD

In the end, Jack gives Lucy the world and a stamp on her passport. Pair each mother and daughter to discuss where they would go if they could take a trip together anywhere in the world. If you have a map of the world, post it where everyone can see. Give each pair a piece of poster paper and markers. They can represent their trip through words, drawing, or both, letting their imaginations be their guides. When all the pairs have finished, tape the

posters up on the walls around the room. Ask each pair to stand next to their poster and discuss it, addressing at least the following:

- Why was this location chosen?
- What would you do and see there?
- What souvenirs would you want to bring home, assuming that money is no object?
- In what ways would your relationship grow through this experience?

After the discussion is finished, ask for volunteers to answer the following:

- Is there a trip you could take to some place closer in which many of these things could occur now?
- What would prevent you from taking such a trip now?

SESSION 3 BEAUTY SLEEP

BACKGROUND
Disney's *Sleeping Beauty* (1959) is 75 minutes long and is rated G.

CAUTIONS Most
audiences will find no objectionable material in this video.

SYNOPSIS When Princess
Aurora is born, the whole kingdom celebrates. But when Maleficent, the mistress of all evil, isn't invited to the party, she curses the tiny baby to die before sundown on her sixteenth birthday. The anguished king and queen send Aurora deep into the forest to live with three good fairies until the time of danger has passed, but Maleficent manages to find her and carry out the wicked spell. Fortunately, the good fairies have countered the evil spell with a spell of their own; and the princess is really just in a deep sleep until she receives her true love's kiss. Brave Prince Phillip must battle all the forces of evil to bestow the kiss, and he and Aurora live happily ever after.

© WALT DISNEY PRODUCTIONS. (COURTESY KOBAL)

LEARN SOMETHING ABOUT EACH OTHER
Separate the mothers from the daughters. The mothers will brainstorm and create a list called "Ten Things You Need to Know to Be a Good Daughter." The daughters will create a list of "Ten Things You Need to Know to Be a Good Mother." After each list is recorded on poster paper and posted, each group will defend its position. Then allow each group to remove one item from the other's

list, while adding an item of its own. This should start the session with some laughs while communicating some basic truths about mother-daughter relationships.

INTRODUCE SLEEPING BEAUTY
Tell the group that the character Aurora had four mothers—her biological mother and three good fairies. Tell the group that like the stories of the featured Scriptures and the other two films, this story is also full of unexpected circumstances and grace-filled relationships. The

participants will notice that the opening scenes reveal that the good fairies may offer one, and only one, wish for the princess. Ask:

- If you could grant just one wish for your daughter or your mother, what would it be? (Tell the group members to hold their thoughts until after the movie. Then they will get the opportunity to reveal their wishes.)

ONE WISH

After the movie, give each mother-daughter team some free time to walk around, preferably outside if space and weather permit. This is the time that mothers and daughters will tell each other their one wish. When they return, ask for volunteers to tell the group about their wishes; but remember to keep this voluntary.

WRAP-UP

Review the definition of the word *grace,* and ask if anyone can remember the examples provided in Scripture and in the movies. Ask:

- What have you learned that you can apply to your own relationships, whether these relationships are with your mother, boyfriend, girlfriend, or other friends and family members?

CLOSE WITH PRAYER

Pray: "Lord, you look into our souls and see the good that is there. You know our potential, our talents, our deep-down goodness. Because you love us with no strings attached, we are free to respond with the same kind of love. You release our potential, and we are newly born. Now help us remember to love others the same way you love us. Teach us, Lord, that we also deserve grace-filled relationships. Teach us to seek out persons who can love us in this way. Thank you for your greatest gift of grace and love, Jesus Christ. It is in his name that we pray. Amen."

TEN COMMANDMENTS
OF USING WEEKEND AT THE MOVIES

Welcome to WEEKEND AT THE MOVIES: THE BEST RETREATS FROM *REEL TO REAL.* The writers, editors, and design team of this youth resource hope that you enjoy the movies as much as we do. And make no mistake, your youth are enjoying and paying attention to the movies. Their gusto for the big (and little) screen presents a perfect opportunity to relate the life, lessons, and good news of Jesus Christ in a current, meaningful, and fun way.

Christian movie lovers have always enjoyed analyzing and discussing religious themes on film. Without a doubt, filmmakers love to incorporate these images and themes. That's why WEEKEND AT THE MOVIES is such a helpful and exciting addition to your youth ministry.

Here are some hints for incorporating the Christian images of film in the lives of your youth. In fact, they are the Ten Commandments of using WEEKEND AT THE MOVIES.

1. Thou shalt always preview the entire film before showing it to thy youth group.
2. Thou shalt always get parental consent before viewing questionable movies (see the Student Movie Pass on the inside back cover).
3. Likewise, thou shalt keep parents well informed of goings-on at all times. Honor thy fathers, mothers, and legal guardians!
4. Thou shalt never infringe upon the Federal Copyright Act (read The Fine Print on page 96).
5. Thou shalt remember—and remind skeptics in thy congregation—that a movie doesn't necessarily have to be a Christian movie to carry Christian messages and themes. Likewise, not all "religious" movies offer Christian messages and themes for thy youth.
6. Thou shalt not think that printed answers to session questions are set in stone. Sometimes there are no right or wrong answers, but WEEKEND AT THE MOVIES offers helpful responses in case the group gets stuck.
7. Thou shalt customize sessions and activities to the personality of thy youth group.
8. Thou shalt use the Video Viewing chart to help thou quickly fast forward to selected movie clips.
9. Thou shalt always preview the entire film before showing it to thy youth group. (OK, we realize that this is the first commandment, but it's *really* important.)
10. Thou shalt have a good time while learning the good news of Jesus Christ.

Serving Our Neighbors
A Lenten or Anytime Retreat Based On The Spitfire Grill and Marvin's Room

THE SPITFIRE GRILL PHOTOS © 1996 CASTLE ROCK ENTERTAINMENT. ALL RIGHTS RESERVED.

We know what love is because Jesus gave his life for us. That's why we must give our lives for each other. If we have all we need and see one of our own people in need, we must have pity on that person, or else we cannot say we love God. Children, you show love for others by truly helping them, and not merely by talking about it.

1 John 3:16-18

MARVIN'S ROOM PHOTOS © 1996 MIRAMAX FILMS. ALL RIGHTS RESERVED.

THEME Christ's suffering represents his love for us. When we accept that love, our own burdens become lighter. And when we imitate that love, we free ourselves to participate in the miracle of rebirth and redemption in Jesus' name.

PURPOSE Youth will learn about the traditions of the Lenten season and experience the spiritual growth that follows the purposeful observance of these traditions.

USING THIS RETREAT
This retreat is a weekend at church or another location large enough to accommodate the group, beginning with Friday dinner and ending with Sunday breakfast before church. The format takes youth through a Lenten season in miniature, beginning with a Mardi Gras party, then proceeding through Ash Wednesday, Maundy Thursday, and finally an Easter sunrise service. The videos explore the Lenten themes of love, suffering, sacrifice, redemption, and rebirth. These themes are ideal for reflection during Lent and also are perfect for study in any part of the Christian year.

VIDEO VIEWING Below are key scenes from *The Spitfire Grill* and *Marvin's Room*. Use the Video Viewing chart for quickly locating these clips during discussion of the films.

Suggestion: Preview the film on the VCR that you will use with the program. Make note of these key scenes so you can fast forward during the program, using these approximate start-end times and your VCR counter.

THE SPITFIRE GRILL

Start-End	Event	Count
1:11–1:13	The town begins its redemption.	_____
1:17–1:22	Eli begins his redemption.	_____
1:42–1:46	Nahum is penitent and redeemed.	_____
1:45–1:51	Percy's sacrifice leads to rebirth and redemption for Claire, Eli, and the town.	_____

MARVIN'S ROOM

Start-End	Event	Count
0:05–0:09	Hank and Charlie before Bessie's love	_____
0:38–0:40	Lee before Bessie's love (There is one strong swear word.)	_____
1:24–1:28	Bessie says that she's been lucky, been able to love.	_____
1:30–End	The family redeemed by Bessie's love	_____

MATERIALS

- *The Spitfire Grill* and *Marvin's Room* videos
- TV and VCR
- Optional: instant camera and film
- Party decorations and music for Mardi Gras and Easter meals
- Food for meals and snacks
- Wall or boards to display photographs and messages; mounting supplies such as tacks or tape; lettering for displays
- Candles, drip guards, matches
- Pit or grill for small outdoor fire, washrags
- Bibles and hymnals
- Concordances or Bible dictionaries

THE MYSTERY OF LENT

Lent is a mystery to most Christians today. If they know anything about it, that knowledge is probably limited to "giving up" something for Lent. We can understand this season better if it is compared with Advent. Advent is a time of preparation and looking outward, watching and waiting for the Christ Child to arrive. It is a time of expectation and preparation, ending with the celebration of Christmas. Lent is also a time of preparation, but in this case the focus is inward. In the process of watching and waiting for the Resurrection Day of Easter, the Christian looks into his or her own soul and reflects on Jesus' great act of love and sacrifice. That is why some people "give up" something during this season. The act reminds them in some small way of Christ's sacrifice. When observed with a prayerful spirit, Lent can be a time of spiritual growth.

DISCUSSING & LEARNING

Begin the first session with a lesson on the meaning of Lent. The word *Lent* is derived from several words meaning "spring," a time when new life and hope abound. However, there is a tendency to think of Lent as a "down" season, concentrating only on sacrifice and not on the outcome. This retreat is designed to balance that picture and provide youth with a more complete image of the season. Use the answers provided and the descriptive article "The Mystery of Lent" to lead the discussion.

Question 1: What is Lent?

Answer 1: Lent is the six weeks before Easter, excluding Sundays, when Christians look inward to contemplate Christ's great sacrifice of love. Lent officially begins on Ash Wednesday and ends on Easter Sunday.

Question 2: Why does Mardi Gras always precede Lent?

Answer 2: Mardi Gras is just one of many festivities around the world during Shrovetide, the time of celebration before the sober Lenten season. In England, Shrove Tuesday is called Pancake Day, when foods that will be denied during Lent are gobbled up. Mardi Gras, or Fat Tuesday, is celebrated in similar style; although in many parts of the world, it has lost its religious significance.

Question 3: Why do people "give up" things for Lent?

Answer 3: When Christians think of Christ's own sacrifice on the cross, they are sometimes motivated to sacrifice something themselves to keep the memory of Christ's act of love alive in their hearts. Food is often chosen because it was not unusual for Jesus to fast during his times of inward contemplation and prayer.

Question 4: What are some other observances during this season?

Answer 4: Ash Wednesday is the first day of Lent. Some Christians participate in a ceremony in which they apply ashes to their forehead, often in the form of a cross, to represent penitence for their sins. Maundy Thursday, the last Thursday before Easter, observes the Last Supper. Just as Jesus washed the disciples' feet on that evening, some Christians perform acts of service on this day.

Question 5: What does Lent have to do with Easter?

Answer 5: While Advent is the season of preparation for Christmas Day, Lent is the season of preparation for Easter Day. During Lent we reflect on Christ's last days and crucifixion so that we may fully appreciate the glory and new birth of the Resurrection.

THE SPITFIRE GRILL

Tell the youth that the movie they are about to see contains many Lenten themes. They need to look for sacrificial love that leads to new birth (or re-creation), inward reflection, redemption, and penitence (feeling sorry) for one's sins.

BACKGROUND

The Spitfire Grill is 110 minutes long and is rated PG-13.

CAUTIONS
This film contains mild profanity, frequent smoking by Percy, and some consumption of alcohol. There is also a frank discussion of sexual abuse and violence to a sixteen-year-old girl.

SYNOPSIS
Twenty-something Percy Talbot is looking for a new life. Upon release from a five-year prison term, she chooses the town of Gilead, Maine, and begins working in crusty old Hannah Ferguson's diner, the Spitfire Grill. She quickly feels the prickly stares and whispers of the town's residents. But Percy is giving by nature; and slowly, through a series of small kindnesses, she begins winning over a few of them.

When Hannah breaks her leg, Percy must take over the diner. Shelby, a shy young mother, steps in to help; and a close friendship results.

However, Shelby's husband Nahum is displeased that an ex-convict is working closely with his Aunt Hannah. Nahum distrusts Percy from the beginning and refuses to give her a chance to redeem herself.

Meanwhile, Percy is developing a relationship with an elusive man who arrives every evening to pick up canned goods that Hannah leaves him behind the Spitfire. When Percy tries to make contact, he first runs, then gradually begins to draw her into his world in the forest.

As the story progresses, Hannah decides to sell the diner; and Percy suggests an essay contest. Each entrant writes an essay explaining why he or she wants to own the diner and accompanies it with $100. The winner gets the diner for $100, and Hannah gets more money than if she had sold it outright. But Nahum thinks that Percy might steal the money; and when he takes it for safekeeping one night, it accidentally winds up in the bag of canned goods that Percy gives to the recluse. Everyone assumes that Percy has stolen the money, giving it to an accomplice in the woods. When Hannah hears that the police are looking for the recluse, she springs Percy from jail. Hannah reveals that the recluse is really her son, Eli, who returned from Vietnam incapable of living a normal life in society. Percy runs after him; and in the attempt to warn him, she drowns.

Retreat Activities

Bible Name Search
The Spitfire Grill uses several biblical names. Have the youth use a Bible dictionary or concordance to look up the following names and then try to connect them to the movie. Here are only a few of the biblical names used in the film. How many more can your group find?

Hannah: Mother of prophet Samuel, so delighted in her son that she dedicated him to God. Hannah Ferguson also has a strong attachment to her son.

Johnny B: John the Baptist, who wore clothing of camel's hair and appeared in the wilderness, resembles the recluse.

Eli: A judge of Israel. There seems to be no connection between the biblical Eli and the character in the movie.

Nahum: The name means "God is compassionate." That was the great lesson the movie Nahum learned.

Gilead: A mountainous country in the Holy Land, east of the Jordan, where a famous healing balm grew. The balm in the video is symbolized by Percy. When the hymn "There Is a Balm in Gilead" is played at her funeral, the people are acknowledging her power to heal sin-sick souls. Jeremiah 8:22 refers to Gilead's balm.

Too late, the town realizes what a treasure Percy was. But there is rebirth. Percy's essay contest brings Claire, a young mother, to Gilead. She receives the fresh start Percy had only dreamed of. And Eli comes in from the woods to begin a relationship with his mother.

DISCUSSING & LEARNING

After viewing the entire movie, lead the youth in a discussion based on the questions below. The Video Viewing chart will help you find key scenes if you would like to view them again.

Question 1: Redemption is a major Lenten theme. To *redeem* means "to pay a price to release someone from a sin or bondage." This is what Christ did for us on the cross; his sacrificial love led to our redemption. In *The Spitfire Grill*, who is redeemed? Who pays the price?

Answer 1: Nearly every character experiences some form of redemption, and it is Percy who pays the price. (Therefore, Percy is a Christ figure.) Hannah is redeemed from her life of angry isolation, Shelby emerges from Nahum's emotional abuse, Nahum is redeemed from his sins of meanness and suspicion, and Eli is freed from his self-imposed imprisonment. Even the town of Gilead is redeemed, because it is transformed from a cluster of cynical gossips to a community of loving neighbors.

Question 2: Love is the greatest power source in the world, because it can radically transform human beings into new creatures. Christ's sacrificial love changed so many individuals that the whole world eventually changed. Percy's sacrificial love did the same thing for a town. Consider the persons who were redeemed in Question 1. Describe their transformation.

Answer 2: Hannah becomes a loving, giving person; Shelby grows strong and able to stand up to her abusive husband; Nahum develops the ability to see his own faults and be less judgmental about the faults of others; Eli overcomes his fears long enough to come out of the woods and make contact with his mother.

Question 3: During Lent we look inward to search for ways in which we have sinned. *Sin* can be defined as "anything that separates us from the love of God." When we find our sins, we feel sorry, or *penitent*. Penitence must come before forgiveness. Identify a scene that clearly portrays penitence.

Answer 3: Although some may point to Hannah's sorrow over blaming Percy for the theft, the strongest example is Nahum's confession at Percy's funeral.

Plant a Seed

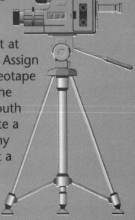

The growth of plants from seeds can symbolize the spiritual growth that can also occur during Lent. Plant seeds or plants, either in small pots or on church grounds, to signify your youth group's faith journey. Remind the youth that just as plants need water and nourishment, their souls also need care. Discuss the kinds of care our souls need.

Plan a Balloon Sunday

First United Methodist Church in Sarasota, Florida, observes the Lenten season by having a party at the main worship service the last Sunday before Ash Wednesday. The sanctuary is filled with hundreds of helium balloons on strings, which are taped to the backs of pews. Special music and a special message give an upbeat note to the event. Ask the youth to plan a balloon Sunday for your church. Consult the pastor for permission, then let the ideas flow.

Make a Video

Allow other youth groups to enjoy a video of this retreat at district gatherings. Assign some youth to videotape major features of the weekend. Other youth can edit it and write a script to accompany the presentation at a later time.

MARVIN'S ROOM

Like *The Spitfire Grill*, *Marvin's Room* abounds with Lenten themes. Ask the youth to watch for themes as they view this film, calling upon the lessons they have learned so far.

BACKGROUND

Marvin's Room is 98 minutes long and is rated PG-13.

CAUTIONS

This movie contains small amounts of profanity and frequent smoking.

SYNOPSIS
Twenty years ago, sisters Lee and Bessie went their separate ways. Lee stayed in Ohio, married, had two sons, divorced, and then raised her sons alone. Bessie moved to Florida after Marvin, their father, had a stroke; and there she remained, caring for him and her slightly dotty old aunt Ruth. Because of that sacrifice, Bessie never had a family of her own. Lee never helped with Marvin; and for this reason, the sisters have lost touch with each other.

But now Bessie has leukemia and needs a bone marrow transplant. Lee and her boys drive to Florida to be tested as donors. Hank, the older son, is angry. He blames Lee for leaving his father and wants to be with his father. Hank burned down their house out of rage and has just been released from a mental institution, where he was sentenced for the crime. Charlie, the younger son, is bookish, quiet, and absorbs all around him without comment.

As the reunited family awaits the results of the tests, their true personalities emerge. Lee is afraid to give love. She feels that she has just started her life and wants no ties to burden her future. Bessie has spent her life giving to others, and this pattern of selfless giving begins to pull on Lee's conscience. Gradually, Lee's heart begins to thaw; and she performs quiet acts of giving that reflect her slowly emerging love for her family. Hank overcomes his anger long enough to love Bessie, then Marvin, and finally his reborn mother.

No donor match is found, and the movie ends with a question mark over Bessie's life. But a miracle has occurred, nevertheless, because Lee has been given a new heart and a family has been healed, all through the power of love.

DISCUSSING & LEARNING

Question 1: It is easy to think of Lent as a time of sacrifice, but that is an incomplete picture. When we sacrifice out of love for others, not out of a sense of obligation, we are transformed by the very love we give. Compare the two sisters. How has Bessie's love shaped the kind of person she has become? How has Lee's selfishness shaped the kind of person she has become?

Answer 1: Bessie is gentle and kind. She smiles constantly and enjoys the companionship of others. Lee seems unable to connect with others, especially her own family. She cannot consider the needs of anyone except herself. She leads a lonely life, filled with activity but with no deep relationships.

Question 2: Near the end of the movie Bessie says that she has been so lucky, that she's had such love in her life. Lee mistakenly believes that Bessie is lucky because Marvin and Ruth have given her love. But what does she really mean?

Answer 2: Bessie means that she is lucky to have been able to love them so much. The love she has given, just as much as the love she has received, has changed her life for the better.

Question 3: Do you agree or disagree with the following statement: "Love is a learned behavior"?

Answer 3: Opinions will vary, but *Marvin's Room* provides evidence that it is true. Through years of practice, Bessie learned how to love. Only after observing and imitating Bessie's acts of kindness did Lee finally begin to learn how to love.

Question 4: Who receives redemption as a result of Bessie's love?

Answer 4: Hank is saved from a life of anger; Lee softens and begins to consider the needs of others; Charlie is saved from a life as a passive onlooker; Marvin and Ruth have also been redeemed to a life of loving care.

Angel Retreat

An Angel Retreat With Sessions Based On *Michael*, *The Preacher's Wife*, and *It's a Wonderful Life*

> For [God] will command his angels concerning you to guard you in all your ways. On their hands they will bear you up, so that you will not dash your foot against a stone.
>
> **Psalm 91:11–12**
>
> I looked up and saw a man clothed in linen, with a belt of gold from Uphaz around his waist. His body was like beryl, his face like lightning, his eyes like flaming torches, his arms and legs like the gleam of burnished bronze, and the sound of his words like the roar of a multitude.
>
> **Daniel 10:5–6**
>
> Do not neglect to show hospitality to strangers, for by doing that some have entertained angels without knowing it.
>
> **Hebrews 13:2**

THEME The Bible is filled with references to angels. Angels also appear in the lives of film characters. In both the Bible and film, angels intervene in different and wonderful ways.

PURPOSE Youth will better understand who and what angels are in Christian theology.

A Basic Theology of Angels

Perhaps the most common contemporary misconception about angels is that human beings "become" angels when they die. Little or no evidence is found in Scripture or Christian tradition to support this point of view. In the Bible angels are seen as a separately created order of spiritual beings. Unlike humans, they are immortal and therefore have no "soul." Like human beings, however, they have free will and can rebel against God (hence Satan and other "fallen angels").

In Scripture angels are most often portrayed as intermediaries between God and humankind and are described as "God's messengers." In fact, the Greek word *angelos,* from which the term *angel* comes, means "messenger." As God's messengers, angels come to inform human beings of God's will for them in the way that the angel Gabriel came to Mary to tell her she had been chosen to bear Jesus. There is also some support for the idea of guardian angels in that angels are often assigned to protect individual human beings or nations.

Many people have suggested that the movie *Michael* implies that angels can have sexual relations with human beings. This, also, is not supported by mainstream tradition. Angels are most often seen as not being of either sex (androgynous). Angels were created by God for joy, not desire; and they are seen as living in such a state of joy that sexuality is not necessary. (The angel in the movie *Michael* can be interpreted as passing on this sense of great joy to all the women, actually everyone, he encounters.)

The "macho" stereotype surrounding angels comes from the idea that "good" angels have been battling "fallen" angels on God's behalf from the time they were created. (This is the source of Michael's need for battle in the movie.)

As Christian theology emphasized the presence of the Holy Spirit and science demanded "proof" of their existence, angels began to diminish in importance and fade from view after the Middle Ages. Now, however, they have made a comeback in a big way. Two of the movies presented here, *The Preacher's Wife* and *It's a Wonderful Life,* support the popular misconception that angels are human beings ascended to a higher order of existence and are assigned to help persons on earth with their problems. There is nothing really wrong about this beautiful notion of angels as an extension of God's loving presence, and it will give you an opportunity to help your youth examine their perspective on angels more completely as you explain to them that historically angels have not been understood this way.

About the Archangel Michael

- Michael has traditionally been revered as God's most highly placed archangel. An archangel is a "chief angel." The Book of Revelation mentions seven archangels, who stand in the presence of the Lord. The four most common angel names associated with the archangels are Michael, Gabriel, Raphael, and Uriel. Of the four, Michael and Gabriel have the most legends associated with them.
- Michael is often referred to as "the chief of all virtue" and "the prince presence." Job descriptions have made him the angel of mercy, righteousness, repentance, and sanctification (the process of becoming holy).
- According to legend, Michael is the one who out-battled Lucifer (Satan) and threw him out of heaven. Legends also suggest that he is the angel to which Revelation refers who binds Satan in the bottomless pit for a thousand years.
- Some legends even suggest that Michael is the angel to whom God has entrusted the keys to the kingdom of heaven. During the Middle Ages, Michael was seen as an escort who accompanied new souls to heaven.
- Michael and Gabriel are the angels who are most often recreated in visual art. Michael is most often depicted as the warrior of God with his sword drawn.
- Most recently, Michael has been discovered in the Dead Sea Scrolls in a book called "The War of the Sons of Light Against the Sons of Darkness" in which he is referred to as the "prince of light" as he battles the forces of darkness.
- The archangel Michael has always been viewed as God's greatest "warrior spirit."

VIDEO VIEWING Begin with an opening prayer. Then view the clips, using the Video Viewing chart below. If you've decided to use both films in their entirety in a lock-in, you might want to have a time for recreation between films, using one of the suggestions in this material, then follow up with the discussion questions after watching the second movie.

Suggestion: Preview the film on the VCR that you will use with the session. Make note of these key scenes so you can fast forward during the program, using these approximate start-end times and your VCR counter.

MICHAEL

Start-End	Event	Count
0:20–0:22	Michael's first appearance	_____
0:24–0:29	Breakfast	_____
0:35–0:39	The trip begins.	_____
0:39–0:41	Battle of the bull	_____
0:46–0:48	Michael's line dance	_____
0:56–0:58	"All You Need Is Love"	_____
1:06–1:09	Dorothy's song	_____
1:17–1:18	"I could forgive you anything."	_____
1:19–1:24	Sparky run down/ Michael's miracle	_____
1:35–End	Quinlan chases Michael and runs into Dorothy.	_____

IT'S A WONDERFUL LIFE

Start-End	Event	Count
0:03–0:05	Prayers for George Bailey	_____
0:05–1:40	George Bailey's life story	_____
1:37–1:39	George's prayer in the bar	_____
1:40–1:45	Contemplating suicide/Clarence's first appearance	_____
1:45–2:02	George wishes he'd never been born.	_____
2:02–2:03	George prays to get his life back.	_____
2:03–2:06	George celebrates his life.	_____
2:06–0:00	George's friends come through for him.	_____
2:10–0:00	Harry's toast	_____
2:10–0:00	"Remember—No man is a failure who has friends."	_____

THE PREACHER'S WIFE

Start-End	Event	Count
0:09–0:11	Henry prays, and Dudley "falls" in.	_____
0:16–0:18	The hold–up takes place.	_____
0:19–0:21	Henry prays again (disbelief).	_____
0:37–0:40	Dudley and Jeremiah talk about Hakim.	_____
0:45–0:47	Joe Hamilton makes an offer to Henry.	_____
0:51–0:54	Henry tells Julia he's accepting the offer.	_____
0:56–1:01	Dudley and Julia go dancing.	_____
1:08–1:10	"You don't believe in much of anything anymore."	_____
1:11–1:12	Prayer is hope.	_____
1:23–1:24	Dudley reminds Henry what is most important.	_____
1:33–1:36	Henry changes his mind.	_____
1:42–1:43	Dudley visits Joe Hamilton.	_____
1:44–1:46	Dudley says goodbye.	_____
1:48–1:52	Henry delivers the Christmas Eve sermon.	_____
1:58–2:00	Jeremiah speaks of faith.	_____

MATERIALS

- *Michael, The Preacher's Wife,* and *It's a Wonderful Life* videos
- TV and VCR
- Whatever is needed for the meals and activities you choose

SESSION 1: MICHAEL

BACKGROUND

Michael (1996) is 106 minutes long and is rated PG.

CAUTIONS As the movie poster said, Michael is an angel, not a saint. He smokes; he drinks beer. It is implied that he has sex (see "A Basic Theology of Angels," page 34, on this point). It is also implied that two other main characters have sex.

SYNOPSIS The archangel Michael, on his last visit to Earth, seeks "to give a man back his heart" and spiritually transforms all those with whom he comes in contact.

DISCUSSING & LEARNING

Question 1: When asked why he doesn't have a halo and an inner light, Michael says he isn't "that kind of angel." What kind of angel is he?

Answer 1: (For help with this one, see the background on angels.)

Question 2: Why does Michael make his new acquaintances take the car trip?

Answer 2: He needs time to bring the joy back into their lives and to accomplish his mission.

Question 3: Why is Michael so obsessed with battle?

Answer 3: He is an archangel, and that is what he has done for most of his existence. After all, he did toss Lucifer from heaven.

Question 4: Michael says, "You gotta learn to laugh; that's the way to true love." Do you agree?

Answer 4: (personal opinion)

ANGEL ACTIVITIES

Angel Food Retreat

Obviously, you will need to have Frosted Flakes® for breakfast; but you can do other creative things with food based on angels or tied to *Michael*. Have an "All Angel" meal.

Serve angel hair pasta and angel food cake. Use an angel cookie cutter to make angel biscuits, cookies, Jell-O® Jigglers, or angel-shaped sandwiches. You could also have a Pie Feast! Make sure that you have all the pies from the movie and have the youth eat and share the pie just as the characters in the movie did.

Angel Line Dance

It shouldn't be difficult for one of the members of your group to learn the moves from the *Michael* Line Dance. Have him or her teach the others, and enjoy an evening of line dancing together.

Question 5: Have someone in the group read aloud Psalm 85. How do you feel this psalm reflects Michael's personality and mission?

Answer 5: (personal opinion)

Question 6: How does Michael help others recover the joy in their lives?

Answer 6: He encourages laughing, dancing, singing, eating pie, listening, caring, and the like.

Question 7: Why does Michael like to see "The World's Largest" stuff?

Answer 7: (personal opinion) Perhaps he wants to remind himself and his companions that there is always something bigger and more important than he is.

Question 8: Listen to Dorothy's song. How does it make you feel?

Answer 8: (personal opinion)

Question 9: Michael says he has a difficult mission, "to give a man back his heart." How does Michael accomplish that mission?

Answer 9: By helping Quinlan understand what is truly important in life and helping him learn to love again (All You Need Is Love!)

Question 10: Quinlan says he could forgive Dorothy anything. Is there anyone in your life whom you feel that way about?

Answer 10: (personal opinion)

SESSION 2: THE PREACHER'S WIFE

BACKGROUND
The Preacher's Wife (1996) is 124 minutes long and is rated PG.

CAUTIONS
None.

SYNOPSIS
God sends the angel Dudley in answer to the prayers of a preacher's family. As Dudley seeks to accomplish his mission, he finds himself becoming attracted to the pastor's wife and is reluctant to leave. In the end Dudley helps everyone he encounters understand the true meaning of Christmas and life.

DISCUSSING & LEARNING
Unless otherwise noted, the responses to the following questions are based on the youth's personal opinion.

Question 1: Henry prays for help, and God sends Dudley. Does God send angels to help us?

Question 2: Why doesn't Henry believe that Billy is innocent of the hold-up?

Question 3: Why doesn't Henry believe that Dudley is an angel? If someone came up and introduced himself or herself as an angel, would you believe him or her?

Answer 3: A fine basis for this discussion is the selected Scripture from Hebrews.

Question 4: Is Dudley the way you envision angels?

Answer 4: For this response, have a youth read the angelic description from the selected Scripture in the Book of Daniel.

All You Need Is Love!
Listen to the Beatles' song "All You Need Is Love" and have everyone sing along. For a laugh, ask lyrically confident members of the youth group to sing "All You Need Is Love" a capella from memory—like Michael did in the movie. Can anyone improve upon Michael's botched rendition? Can anyone be worse? Have a contest for the most accurate and the most distorted renditions.

Commission the Youth as an "Angel Corps"
Michael's mission was to "give a man back his heart." If the youth group become angels, how can they work to give people back their

hearts? Assign each youth a specific "ministry task" or help him or her choose his or her own.

Question 5: Is your pastor as overworked and underappreciated as Henry?

Question 6: Why does Henry decide to accept Joe Hamilton's offer at first?

Question 7: Why doesn't Henry let Dudley do the pastoral errands and go dancing with his wife?

Question 8: Is it possible for a pastor like Henry to do so many good things for people and still have lost his ability to believe and have faith?

Question 9: Do you agree that prayer is like shooting a basketball and watching it go through the net? Do you believe that "prayer is hope"?

Question 10: Have you ever come to a place in your life where you have forgotten what is important and lost your way? Who helped you find your way back?

Question 11: Dudley tells Henry that St. Matt's is "the glue that holds this neighborhood together and without it the neighborhood will fall." Do you feel the same way about your church?

Question 12: What is a miracle? Is Joe Hamilton's change of heart a miracle? Is Henry's change of heart a miracle?

In his sermon, Henry says that "the miracle is when we love someone we are really loving God." (You might point this out as the youth answer the next question.)

Question 13: Listen to Henry's Christmas Eve sermon. What essential things does he have to say about forgiveness, hope, love, and Christianity?

ACTION POINT

Have your youth group spearhead a Pastor Appreciation Sunday. During a worship service, recognize your pastor's dedication. Have a dinner in honor of the pastor and his or her family. Fill a bulletin board with pictures of his or her compassion in action. Give testimonies of the way your lives have been touched by the pastor in his or her presence. Write letters and send cards that express gratitude and appreciation. Arrange for him or her to receive a note of encouragement from a member of the youth group each day for a month (or longer). Have a fundraiser to do something special for him or her and his or her family (an all-expenses paid, three-day weekend for the pastoral family or that laptop computer he or she needs and wants but cannot afford). The possibilities are limitless.

SESSION 3: *IT'S A WONDERFUL LIFE*

BACKGROUND

It's a Wonderful Life (1946) is 125 minutes long. It was made before the rating system but would be rated G. The best video version, by far, is the Republic Pictures Family Collection 50th Anniversary Edition (original uncut version, remastered, 1996).

CAUTIONS
None. This is a perfect family movie.

SYNOPSIS
When George Bailey is faced with a crisis he cannot bear, he contemplates suicide. The angel Clarence is sent to help him and grants his wish that he had never been born. George sees the world, for the first time, as it would be if he had not touched all the lives around him. Clarence's action enables George to decide that it is a wonderful life and that he wants to live, no matter what the consequences. His friends come through for him, and he celebrates the true meaning of life with them.

DISCUSSING & LEARNING
Unless otherwise noted, the responses to the following questions are based on the youth's personal opinions.

Question 1: Why does George Bailey want to end his life?

Answer 1: He and his building and loan business are having big financial troubles.

Question 2: Have you ever been this desperate? Have you ever known someone who was this desperate?

Answer 2: Since this is a sensitive subject for teens, pose this as a rhetorical question. Do not pressure anyone for a response; rather, discuss the desperate feeling of "it would be a better world without me."

Question 3: Is Clarence the kind of angel you would want God to send to take care of you? What are his good qualities?

Question 4: This film begins with everyone in town praying for George Bailey. How does God answer our prayers? Tell the group about a time when you felt that your prayers were answered by God.

Question 5: Have you ever felt that an angel was watching over you?

Question 6: George gets a chance to see the world as it would be if he had never been born. How would the world be different if you had not been born? Can you name a person whose life would be less full if you were not around to love him or her?

Question 7: George's friends come through for him in a crisis even though he didn't inform them of his problem. Do you have someone with whom you can share your problems? Has there been a time when your friends came through for you?

Question 8: Do you know someone like George Bailey—someone who always thinks about others before he or she thinks about himself or herself?

Question 9: George gives up everything—his plans to travel, his plans to go to college, his plans for the future, and even his honeymoon—for other people. Would you be able to make those kinds of sacrifices for the people you love?

Question 10: Clarence inscribes his gift to George with the following words: "Remember—no man is a failure who has friends." Do you agree?

Question 11: Has the way you see angels changed during this retreat? If so, how?

The Michael Quiz
Answers & Questions

The following answers (and questions) can be asked of your group in a Jeopardy®-like format featuring either individuals or teams. Be sure to have noisemakers that will allow participants to buzz in.

A Where Michael is staying when he is "discovered" by tabloid reporters
Q What is the Milk Bottle Motel?

A The name of the bank Michael "smites" for Pansy
Q What is the 1st Iowa Bank of Commerce, Stubbs Branch?

A "Moneychanger, I shall turn this earthly den into a parking lot."
Q What Michael says when he smites the bank

A Michael sees or has seen these four "world's largest" things. (One he mentions and the others he actually sees in the movie.)
Q What are the World's Largest Cannonball, the World's Largest Ball of Twine, the World's Largest Non-Stick Frying Pan, the World's Tallest Building?

A The location of the World's Largest Cannonball
Q What is Mesopotamia?

A The location of the World's Largest Non-Stick Frying Pan
Q What is Meansboro?

A The World's Tallest Building and its location
Q What is the Sears Tower in Chicago?

A The height of the World's Tallest Building
Q What is 1,454 feet above street level?

A The circumference of the World's Largest Ball of Twine
Q What is 45 feet?

A The dog in *Michael*
Q Who is Sparky?

A The opposite of white
Q What is yolk?

A The tabloid newspaper for which Huey, Quinlan, and Dorothy work
Q What is the *National Mirror*?

A Dorothy claims to be an expert in these.
Q What are angels?

A The names of Dorothy Winters' three ex-husbands
Q Who are Bradley, Miles, and Ralph?

A The first Sparky died here.
Q What is underneath a tractor tire?

A Michael says that you can never get too much of this, even on your Frosted Flakes®.
Q What is sugar?

A Michael is staying with her at the beginning of the movie.
Q Who is Pansy Milbank?

A Pansy is cooking this meal when she dies.
Q What is breakfast?

A Michael is allowed this many visits.
Q What is 26?

A The three smells women associate with Michael
Q What are cookies, caramel, and cotton candy?

A Michael's brand of cereal
Q What is Kellogg's Frosted Flakes®?

A Michael claims it's why he doesn't have a halo and an inner light.
Q What is "I'm not that kind of angel"?

A Michael battled and threw this figure from heaven.
Q Who is Lucifer?

A Don't call Michael this nickname.
Q What is Mike?

A Quinlan gives Michael this article of clothing before they begin the drive to Chicago.
Q What is his raincoat?

A Quinlan's promise to Michael
Q What is apologize when Michael asks him to?

A Dorothy's promise to Michael
Q What is to sing?

A Pansy leaves this game for the road trip.
Q What is car bingo?

A Michael's way of eating a lemon
Q What is by making lemonade?

A Michael wrote this psalm.
Q What is Psalm 85?

A Some of Michael's inventions.
Q What are standing in line, marriage, and (he jokes) pie?

A At least three kinds of pie served at the second restaurant
Q What are apple, banana cream, coconut cream, sour cream raisin, chocolate cream, key lime, strawberry rhubarb, lemon meringue, key lime?

A Michael line dances to this song with the women at the bar.
Q What is "Chain of Fools"?

A The jail guard says he has this peculiar creature in his yard.
Q What is a two-headed chicken?

A The book from which Michael reads about the world's largest stuff
Q What is *Amazing America*?

A The title of Dorothy's country song
Q What is "Sitting on the Side of the Road in the Middle of Nowhere"?

OTHER ANGEL FILMS WORTH NOTING

- *Almost an Angel* (1990) gives us Paul Hogan (*Crocodile Dundee*) as a repentant thief who is killed in a car accident and gets a chance to redeem himself by doing angelic good deeds.

- *Always* (1989) is an angelic romance, featuring Richard Dreyfuss as a risk-taking pilot who is killed sacrificing himself to save a friend as he fights forest fires. His first assignment is to become the guardian angel of an inexperienced pilot who will steal his girlfriend's heart. This is a remake of the excellent 1944 flick *A Guy Named Joe,* which features the incomparable Spencer Tracy.

- *The Bishop's Wife* (1947), starring Cary Grant, is the film on which *The Preacher's Wife* is based.

- *Angels in the Outfield* (1994) gives us Danny Glover as a baseball manager who is taught the meaning of life by the angels who aid his team and by the love of a little boy. This is a remake of the exceptional 1951 flick by the same name.

- *Angel on My Shoulder* (1946) is another great '40s flick, which features Paul Muni as a gangster who makes a deal with the devil in order to return to earth and set things straight.

- *Wings of Desire* (1988) is a breathtakingly beautiful motion picture directed by Wim Wenders. The story follows an angel who spends his time observing humankind only to fall in love and reenter the world as a mortal human, giving up his angelic immortality in the balance.
- *Faraway, So Close!* (1993), another film by Wim Wenders, tells the story of another angel who decides to become human but fails to find happiness.

- *Heaven Can Wait* (1978) is a movie about a quarterback who is mistakenly taken to heaven before his time by a rookie angel. They search together for a suitable body to replace his original body. Yet another remake of a great 1943 flick of the same name, this time both films owe everything to *Here Comes Mr. Jordan* (1941), which stars Claude Rains and Robert Montgomery.

- *Waiting for the Light* (1990) tells the story of an angel who takes up residence at a run-down, small-town diner during the Cuban missile crisis. The angel quickly becomes a sensation, and the lives of all involved are transformed by his presence.

ANGEL RESOURCES

- *Angels, A to Z* (Gale Research, Inc., 1995) by James R. Lewis and Evelyn Dorothy Oliver is an excellent choice if you were going to own only one book about angels. This book also includes a detailed bibliography of other angel-related books, films, and resources.

- *The Interpreter's Dictionary of the Bible, Volume 1* (Abingdon Press, 1976) provides an excellent background on the Judeo–Christian understanding of angels.

- Gustav Davidson has collected excellent short biographies describing angels from the Bible, legend, and folklore in *A Dictionary of Angels: Including the Fallen Angels* (Free Press, 1994).

- If you are looking for a much more in-depth treatment of the theology surrounding angels (and we do mean *in depth*), Stuart Schneiderman's *An Angel Passes: How the Sexes Became Divided* (New York University Press, 1988) would be a good choice.

Be careful about your choice of other angel resources as many of them are presented through New Age rather than Christian theology.

The Wizard of Oz CONNECTION

L et's start with the dog. Doesn't Sparky look just a wee bit like Toto? Then, did you notice that twister at the beginning? Next, the four companions (five companions if you count Toto—er, I mean Sparky) are on the road, on a quest, seeing many unusual sights and singing every now and then. Also there are constant reminders that someone (the mean tabloid editor) is trying to take Sparky away.

Quinlan needs to find a heart (the tin man); Huey claims he doesn't have a brain in his head (the scarecrow); and Michael is trying to summon the courage to complete his mission, leaving the earth behind forever, never to return (the lion). Oh, and what is the leading lady's name? Why, Dorothy, of course!

Coincidence? I think not!

The Heavenly Retreat

Once Jesus was asked by the Pharisees when the kingdom of God was coming, and he answered, "The kingdom of God is not coming with things that can be observed; nor will they say, 'Look, here it is!' or 'There it is!' For, in fact, the kingdom of God is among you."

Luke 17:20-21

THEME
God has promised that we will have eternal life in heaven. But what is heaven like?

PURPOSE
The youth will explore a multitude of ideas about the nature of heaven and the afterlife as a foundation for expressing their own theological understanding of what heaven is like.

BACKGROUND
City of Angels (1998) is 114 minutes long and is rated PG-13, *Defending Your Life* (1991) is 112 minutes long and is rated PG, *Always* (1989) is 106 minutes long and is rated PG, *Ghost* (1990) is 128 minutes long and is rated PG-13, and *Heaven* (1987) is a documentary that is 88 minutes long and rated PG-13.

CAUTIONS
There are some mild instances of language and sexual innuendo in these movies (for instance, the famous "potter's wheel" scene in *Ghost*). *Heaven* contains some references to the possibility of sexuality in heaven. *Defending Your Life* has some theology that could be termed New Age; so be prepared to help the youth interpret those ideas from a Christian perspective (for instance, reincarnation is presented as part of the divine plan; but in any discussion of heaven in a youth group setting in the '90s, someone will invariably bring up that subject for discussion anyway).

SYNOPSES
City of Angels is the story of an angel who spends his time observing humankind, only to fall in love and reenter the world as a human being, giving up his angelic immortality for the woman he loves. It is based on the classic German film *Wings of Desire,* directed by Wim Wenders.

Defending Your Life is a comedy about a man who is killed in a car accident and finds himself in Judgment City, defending his life before he can move on to whatever is next.

Always is an angelic romance about a risk-taking pilot who sacrifices himself to save a friend as he fights forest fires. His first assignment in the afterlife is to become the guardian angel of an inexperienced pilot, who will steal his girlfriend's heart. This is a remake of the excellent 1944 flick *A Guy Named Joe,* which features the incomparable Spencer Tracy.

Ghost is the story of a man who is murdered; and rather than move on to heaven, he stays with the woman he loves. Whoopi Goldberg won an Oscar® for her role as a psychic medium who helps the couple communicate and solve the crime.

Heaven is an excellent documentary directed by Diane Keaton, featuring interviews centered around several of the most pressing questions about the nature of heaven and what people believe about heaven. Each question is accented with clips from classic films.

MATERIALS

- *City of Angels* video
- *Defending Your Life* video
- One or more videos of the following films to supplement the other two: *Always, Ghost,* and *Heaven* (You may even choose one of the older versions of these films if you wish.)
- TV and VCR
- Bibles
- Concordances

CENTRAL SESSION: WHAT IS HEAVEN LIKE?

BEFORE THE SESSION
This session is intended to take place after all the films have been viewed in their entirety. After each of the movies you have chosen to use for your retreat, you will have a discussion about the images of heaven that are presented by that film. Guidelines are provided for the discussion of each individual film's "idea of heaven" following this central session.

HEAVENLY ACTIVITY
Divide the youth into groups of six to eight. Give each group a concordance and and some Bibles. Have the youth look up all the places where the word *heaven* appears in the New Testament. (You do need to stick to the New Testament in this case.) You may want to divide up the references equally before the session so that each group has a particular book of the Bible in which to look. Have the youth write down their favorite passages about heaven to tell the group.

HEAVENLY BRAINSTORM
After reviewing what the Scriptures have to say, lead the group in a brainstorming session about the images of heaven presented in the Bible; the films of this retreat; and popular culture, in general. These may include but are not limited to a heavenly city as described in Revelation, a specific city spiritualized (the new Jerusalem), a garden paradise (a new Eden), a place of judgment, a place where we go to learn and progress to even higher states of being, the courtroom of a king, an idealized version of our present existence, a beautiful heavenly "field," earth "recreated" as heaven, a heavenly "home," "mansions of glory," a place of pure light and/or love, a spiritual reality that cannot be described in human terms, a choir of angels, "oneness with God," and so forth. Ask the youth which of these concepts of heaven are most appealing to them. Have them describe why a specific concept of heaven gives them assurance and comfort.

HEAVENLY BIBLE STUDY

Then he began to speak, and taught them, saying: "Blessed are the poor in spirit, for theirs is the kingdom of heaven. "Blessed are those who mourn, for they will be comforted. "Blessed are the meek, for they will inherit the earth. "Blessed are those who hunger and thirst for righteousness, for they will be filled. "Blessed are the merciful, for they will receive mercy. "Blessed are the pure in heart, for they will see God. "Blessed are the peacemakers, for they will be called children of God. "Blessed are those who are persecuted for righteousness' sake, for theirs is the kingdom of heaven. "Blessed are you when people revile you and persecute you and utter all kinds of evil against you falsely on my account. Rejoice and be glad, for your reward is great in heaven, for in the same way they persecuted the prophets who were before you.

(The Beatitudes)

Matthew 5:2-12

Say: "In his wonderful book *Afterlife: The Other side of Dying,* Morton Kelsey has pointed out that the Beatitudes are about the spiritual nature of heaven. We have discussed several possibilities for the way that heaven can be visualized. Now we need to focus on heaven as spiritual reality. Notice that the reward in the first beatitude and the last is the same: 'for theirs is the kingdom of heaven.' The promises of these two verses enclose the others. Kelsey has suggested that the six statements in between give us Jesus' description of what heaven is like. The qualities of this spiritual reality as described by Jesus are as follows: *humility* (poor in spirit), *comfort* (for those who mourn), *gentleness* (those who are meek), *mercy* and *forgiveness* (the merciful), *pure love* (pure in heart), and *peace* (peacemakers). The final statement is about perseverance even when the world despises you." Lead the youth in a discussion of the Beatitudes as a description of the spiritual qualities of heaven. Emphasize the passage from Luke 17:20-21—"The kingdom of God is among you."

Have the youth read 1 Corinthians 15:44b-58 and discuss it at length. In this passage, Paul differentiates between what is physical and what is spiritual. Paul makes it clear that we don't know the details of how we will be changed when we go to heaven (that's the mystery), but we will be changed into an immortal, imperishable existence.

DISCUSSING & LEARNING: CITY OF ANGELS

But someone has testified somewhere, "What are human beings that you are mindful of them, or mortals, that you care for them? You have made them for a little while lower than the angels; you have crowned them with glory and honor."

Hebrews 2:6-7

Question 1: In *City of Angels,* the angels are not in heaven; but they are part of an eternal reality. What do they have that we don't have? (*eternal life; ability to comprehend all languages, to hear thoughts, to hear music in the sunrise and sunset; a special knowledge of God*) What do we have that they don't have? (*touch, taste, pain, love, relationships*) Do you think that any or all of these qualities are part of what heaven is?

Question 2: The angels hear music in the sunrise and sunset. Do you think that there is beauty out there that we cannot experience on this level of existence?

Question 3: In the opening scenes, Seth comes to take the little girl; and she asks, "Where are we going?" Seth answers, "Home." What does this tell you about the nature of heaven? What do we mean when we call heaven "home"?

Question 4: When Seth perceives that Maggie is in despair over the loss of her patient, he tells her, "He is living—just not the way you think." Maggie replies, "I don't believe in that." Then Seth says, "Some things are true whether you believe them or not." Why do you think some people have a problem believing in heaven? Have you ever doubted the existence of heaven?

Question 5: Because he was also once an angel, Nathan Messinger senses that Seth is in his room. Nathan says: "I can't see ya, but I know you're there." Do you believe that there are spiritual and heavenly realities all around us that we cannot comprehend with our physical senses?

Question 6: The angels observe all that goes on all over the earth and take notes. Do you think that we will be aware of what is going on on earth when we are in heaven? Would you want to know?

Question 7: Nathan Messinger says to Maggie: "Seth knows no fear, no pain, no hunger. He hears music in the sunrise; but he'd give up eternity for you." And when Seth's friend Cassiel asks him: "If you had known [she would die], would you have done it?" Seth replies, "I would rather have had one breath of her hair, one kiss of her mouth, one touch of her hand, than an eternity without it." What do you think this says about eternal life? (*Love is the single most important aspect of eternal life in heaven.*)

DISCUSSING & LEARNING: DEFENDING YOUR LIFE

> Then I saw a new heaven and a new earth; for the first heaven and the first earth had passed away, and the sea was no more. And I saw the holy city, the new Jerusalem, coming down out of heaven from God, prepared as a bride adorned for her husband.
>
> **Revelation 21:1-2**

(Revelation Chapters 21–22 describe the heavenly city in detail).

> Love has been perfected among us in this: that we may have boldness on the day of judgment, because as he is, so are we in this world. There is no fear in love, but perfect love casts out fear; for fear has to do with punishment, and whoever fears has not reached perfection in love.
>
> **1 John 4:17-18**

Question 1: How do you feel about the idea of being transported to a Judgment City, where you will stand trial and have to defend the way you have lived your life?

Question 2: Could you imagine heaven as a city like this?

Question 3: Do you feel that the descriptions of heaven as a city in Revelation describe the way heaven literally will be? Or do you think that John was simply using the most beautiful aspects of this world to describe the inexpressible beauty of the next?

Question 4: Daniel's lawyer, Bob Diamond, talks about "little brains" and "big brains." Do you think that what you know and what you still have to learn are important parts of progressing to heaven?

Question 5: What does Daniel need to overcome in the process of "defending his life"? (his fears)

Question 6: What are Daniel's fears? (These would include, but not be limited to, fear of failure, fear of not living up to other people's expectations, fear that he is not good enough to be loved by a person like Julia, fear of judgment, fear of what other people think about him and his behavior, and so forth.)

Question 7: What do you fear spiritually?

Question 8: Read the Scripture verses from First John. In what ways does fear hold us back from the perfect expression of love?

Question 9: How does Daniel overcome his fear? (He falls in love with Julia and has to conquer his fear in order to be with her.) Emphasize verse 18: "There is no fear in love, but perfect love casts out fear; for fear has to do with punishment, and whoever fears has not reached perfection in love." Do you think of yourself as being in the process of being perfected in the love of God?

Question 10: Based on where you are in your spiritual journey today, if you were asked to defend your life, would you feel worthy of heaven? (Tell the youth that salvation comes through the grace of Jesus Christ and that works or good deeds are our response to that loving forgiveness.)

DISCUSSING & LEARNING: ALWAYS

Those who find their life will lose it, and those who lose their life for my sake will find it.

Matthew 10:39

Question 1: When Pete dies, he is transported to a section of wilderness that has been burned out in a forest fire. As he wanders, he finds a spot that is lush green and filled with flowers. There he meets his mentor, Hap. She tells him that he has work to do before he can move on to heaven. How do you feel about this vision of the afterlife?

Question 2: Hap tells Pete that anything he does for himself from here on out is wasted effort. Do you believe that getting rid of all your self-centered concerns is necessary for you to go to heaven?

Question 3: Pete has the difficult task of separating himself from the woman he loves so that he can move on to heaven. Hap tells him that he needs to let his connection to this life go in order to be in heaven. Would you be able to let your world go if you had to go to heaven today?

Question 4: What does Pete finally realize about his relationships with Dorinda, Al, and Ted? (He realizes that his love will always be with them and that their love will go with him.)

Question 5: Read aloud Matthew 10:39. How does Pete "lose his life" in order to find it?

EVERYTHING YOU EVER WANTED TO KNOW ABOUT HEAVEN (BUT WERE AFRAID TO ASK)

For more information and some in-depth (and we do mean in-depth) reading, check out *Heaven: A History*, by Colleen McDannell and Bernard Lang; and *Afterlife: The Other Side of Dying*, by Morton Kelsey. And C.S. Lewis considers heaven in his famous work *The Great Divorce*.

WHAT DREAMS MAY COME

This film about heaven starring Robin Williams is rated PG-13 mostly for thematic elements that involve death and graphic (and potentially disturbing) elements of hell. See Vol. 3, No. 1 of *Reel to Real* for a discussion of this movie.

DISCUSSING & LEARNING: *GHOST*

But as for you, man of God, shun all this; pursue righteousness, godliness, faith, love, endurance, gentleness. Fight the good fight of the faith; take hold of the eternal life, to which you were called and for which you made the good confession in the presence of many witnesses.

1 Timothy 6:11-12

Question 1: Sam gives up his first chance to go to heaven in order to stay with Molly. Would you be able to do that? What if he never had another opportunity?

Question 2: Read 1 Timothy 6:11-12. How does Sam "fight the good fight of the faith"? Does he exhibit all the qualities listed here?

Question 3: How do you feel about the shadow creatures rising up to take the bad guys off to judgment? Is this part of your understanding of the afterlife?

Question 4: When the angels come for those going to heaven, they come in a tunnel of light. Many near-death experiences describe going to heaven as traveling up a tunnel of light. How do you feel about this image?

Question 5: Read John 1:1-10, emphasizing verse 5: "The light shines in the darkness, and the darkness did not overcome it." When the light comes for Sam, in the background you can just barely make out the images of other souls waiting for him to cross over. They appear as beings of pure light. How do you feel about this image of heaven?

Question 6: As Sam begins to leave, he tells Molly, "It's amazing—the love inside—you take it with you." Do you believe that our love here gives us a hint of what heaven will be like and feel like?

HEAVEN

Diane Keaton's documentary, *Heaven*, would be an excellent addition to your Heavenly Retreat. The film itself is an edited montage of responses to interviews Keaton did with a variety of people. Those interviewed range from "normal" folks to eccentric ones. She also interviews evangelists, preachers, members of the Salvation Army, and several people who profess to have "special knowledge" of heaven.

Throughout these excerpts from interviews, Keaton places footage from rare classic films that feature various images of heaven. Especially intriguing is an extended montage (about 39 minutes into the film) in which we are treated to images of heavenly escalators, heavenly gardens, fields of clouds, heavenly cities, angel choirs, and heavenly courts.

This film could be used alone in a mini-retreat on the subject of heaven, as the responses from the interviews are organized around the most pressing questions about heaven: Are you afraid to die? What is heaven? Do you believe in heaven? Can heaven be here on earth? Have you had visions? What is God like? Is there love in heaven? What are the rewards of heaven? Can you prove there is a heaven? How do you get to heaven? (*Pause after each question for discussion with your group.*)

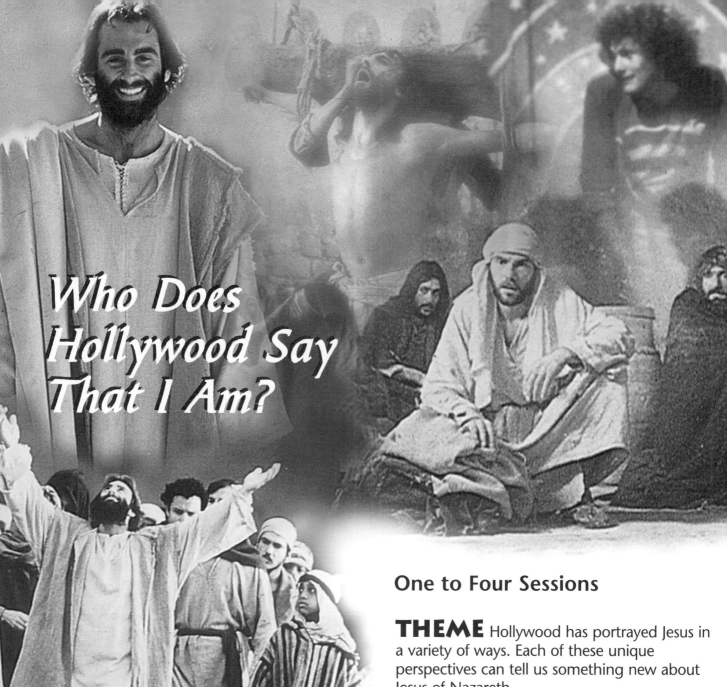

Who Does Hollywood Say That I Am?

Jesus went on with his disciples to the villages of Caesarea Philippi; and on the way he asked his disciples, "Who do people say that I am?" And they answered him, "John the Baptist; and others, Elijah; and still others, one of the prophets." He asked them, "But who do you say that I am?" Peter answered him, "You are the Messiah."

Mark 8:27-29

One to Four Sessions

THEME Hollywood has portrayed Jesus in a variety of ways. Each of these unique perspectives can tell us something new about Jesus of Nazareth.

PURPOSE Youth will begin to develop their own understanding of who Jesus is.

BACKGROUND *Godspell* is 101 minutes long and is rated G; *The Gospel According to Matthew* is 4 hours long and is not rated (would be G); *Jesus of Nazareth* is 6 hours long and is not rated (would be G); *Jesus* is 118 minutes long and is rated G.

CAUTIONS There are no objectionable elements in these four films, although the depiction of the Crucifixion (not used for these sessions) is graphically violent in all but *Godspell*.

MATERIALS

- Videos of the four films
- TV and VCR
- Pictures of Jesus, collections of images of Jesus
- Hymnals
- Art materials and junk items

Note: The films should be available at your local video or Christian resource center. If not, see "Finding the Films," page 53.

SYNOPSES
Jesus selects episodes from the life of Christ only from the Gospel of Luke. *The Gospel According to Matthew* is just what the title implies. As the text of the New International Version of Matthew's Gospel is read, actors dramatize the action and speak the dialogue. *Jesus of Nazareth* is a TV miniseries combining episodes from all four Gospels as well as adding fictional scenes, such as those involving Zealots and scheming priests. *Godspell* stands apart in that it, like *Jesus Christ, Superstar,* is not a depiction of the historical Jesus but a Jesus-transformed musical, set in contemporary New York City. Jesus is depicted as the leader of a troupe of miming clowns bringing joy and faith into an oppressively drab, unfriendly city.

USING THESE SESSIONS & ACTIVITIES

The study is designed for one to four sessions and could easily run to more or be used to fill a weekend retreat. A different aspect of the life of Jesus was chosen from each film for each session. Some groups might want to focus on the same event, as seen from different films' perspectives.

The movie comparison chart on pages 50–51 lists parallel events and their approximate times on film. *Jesus Christ, Superstar* is included as an insightful and entertaining rock musical option. (See overview of the movie at right.)

© 1973 BRIDGESTONE MULTIMEDIA

SESSION 1: GODSPELL— JESUS AS A JOY-BRINGING CLOWN

Have pictures of Jesus displayed on the walls and/or have books of images of Christ from various cultures on tables. Encourage early arrivals to look over these items. Begin by praying or singing "Day by Day" from *Godspell.* (The words are in many hymnals and on the *Godspell* soundtrack.)

Say: "Artists have always been fascinated by Jesus, with each artist creating an image that reflects his or her belief and unique understanding about Jesus. Filmmakers are no exception. Passion plays have been put to film for the entertainment and inspiration of audiences since the beginning of filmmaking. We will view short portions of four movies about Jesus. Just as people centuries ago were both inspired and challenged by certain images of Jesus, so also audiences today react to new films depicting the Savior. Every artistic portrayal of Jesus is one person's attempt to answer the question Jesus put to the disciples in Mark 8:27-31: 'Who do people say that I am?' "

More than 25 years ago, two graduate students in Pittsburgh wrote a musical based on the life of Jesus set in present-day America, which came to be known as *Godspell.* In 1973 both *Godspell* and *Jesus Christ, Superstar* burst onto the scene with challenging visions of who Jesus was. Both films were surrounded by controversy. *Godspell*'s "Christ as Clown" was hard for some to accept, as was the rock format of *Jesus Christ, Superstar.* Both were criticized for their portrayal (or, as some argued, lack of portrayal) of the Resurrection.

Show the video clips up to the scene where Jesus puts on the Superman shirt (approximately 14 minutes) or up to the scene where all the disciples put on costumes (approximately 19 minutes).

Question 1: How do the disciples seem at first? Is theirs a friendly city? What do you think of transposing the story of Jesus on a modern American city?

Answer 1: Note the stark contrast between urban New York City of *Godspell* and historical rural Galilee. This contrast may dictate the disciples' outlook and attitude.

Jesus Christ, Superstar

The movie version of Andrew Lloyd Webber and Tim Rice's rock opera centered on the last seven days of Jesus' life and became the focus of intense controversy from the moment it was released in 1973. Protested as a blasphemous, "hippie" version of the gospel that emphasized the humanity of Jesus rather than his divinity, it became a starting point for discussions about how God was present in Jesus of Nazareth. Despite the protests, many people credit *Jesus Christ, Superstar* for bringing them back to Christianity by offering them a unique perspective of the person and power of Jesus Christ. If you show parts of this film to your youth, they will be both amused by dated styles and costumes and impressed by the power of the performances.

Question 2: What do you think of this portrayal of Jesus leading a troupe of clowns? What is the role or purpose of a clown?

Answer 2: To bring joy and laughter to others; to humor and humble the pretentious and powerful

Question 3: Do you see a connection between the role of a clown and the role of Jesus?

Answer 3: Jesus poked fun at the Pharisees in the Sermon on the Mount. He also attacked the rich and powerful.

Question 4: How is the song during Jesus' baptism, "When Wilt Thou Save the People," appropriate at this point?

Answer 4: John's preaching and baptism of Jesus is an answer to the question in the song; and Jesus' name means "Yahweh (God) saves."

Jesus and the Four Kinds of Clowns

The **parade clown**'s job is to help people join the parade. Parade clowns reach out and touch the crowd in the same way that Jesus urged his followers to become part of the gospel. The **circus clown**'s job is to draw attention away from failure. When the trapeze artist falls, the circus clowns come streaming out to give the performer time to get back up to the bar. This parallels the grace and redemption that Jesus brings to each of us. The **fool**'s or **jester**'s role is to help remove the stress from serious situations by making fun of them. Jesters performed for kings and queens, through their humor, telling the truth that no one else could tell straightforward. Finally, there is the **rodeo clown**. The rodeo clown's job is to stand between the rodeo rider and death itself. When the rider falls from a horse or bull, the rodeo clowns draw the rage of the animal toward themselves to allow the rider to get to safety. This parallels Jesus' death on the cross for each of us.

The Quick and Easy "Who Does Hollywood Say That I Am?"

The approximate start times (hour:minute) are listed for each scene. For *The Gospel According to Matthew*, the numbers

Scenes	Godspell	The Gospel According to Matthew
1. Jesus and John the Baptist	1. 0:10	1. Tape 1, Matthew 3:1-17
2. Jesus calls the disciples.	2. Start	2. Tape 1, Matthew 4:17-22
3. Jesus preaches.	3. 0:44	3. Tape 1, Matthew 5:1-16
4. Jesus teaches.	4. 0:58	4. Tape 2, Matthew 13:1-23
5. Jesus heals.	5. —	5. Tape 2, Matthew 9:18-26
6. Jesus shows anger.	6. 0:08	6. Tape 3, Matthew 21:12-17
7. The garden of Gethsemane	7. 0:25	7. Tape 4, Matthew 26:36-46
8. The Crucifixion	8. 0:32	8. Tape 4, Matthew 27:32-56
9. The Resurrection	9. 0:36	9. Tape 4, Matthew 28:1-10

COURTESY OF THE VISUAL BIBLE

Question 1: Jesus walks around in the crowd while he is speaking this sermon. Is this different from the way you have envisioned Jesus delivering the Sermon on the Mount? Why do you think he is shown doing this?

Answer 1: Traditional paintings and most films show Jesus seated or standing on the mountain above the crowd. The filmmakers want to make the scene more engaging by showing Jesus interacting with more people in a lively way. Notice, for instance, that Jesus takes off his outer garment and gives it away.

Question 2: Jesus teaches his listeners to turn the other cheek when attacked and to love their enemies and pray for those who persecute them. Is this easy to do, or does it even seem foolish?

Answer 2: Of course, it is not easy; and many have claimed that it is foolish to act this way. Most of the action movies you see teach the opposite—kill your enemy before the enemy kills you.

SESSION 2: *THE GOSPEL ACCORDING TO MATTHEW—A LAUGHING JESUS*

This film is more traditional in that it is a dramatized version of the text of the Gospel of Matthew. Yet, some of Jesus' actions in this film are anything but traditional. This Jesus obviously enjoys life and is fun to be around. And, of all times and places, it is while Jesus is preaching the Sermon on the Mount that we see some of Jesus' playfulness displayed.

Rather than indicating a time or a scene for viewing scenes in this video, the reference points in *The Gospel According to Matthew* are chapter and verses. These biblical reference points appear at the lower right of the screen through all four tapes, making it easy to find any scene and to match it to your Bible.

Jesus Movie Comparison Chart
refer to the chapter and verse references, which appear at the bottom right of the television screen.

Scenes	Jesus of Nazareth	Jesus	Jesus Christ, Superstar*
1. Jesus and John the Baptist	1. Tape 1, 1:39	1. 0:08	1. —
2. Jesus calls the disciples.	2. Tape 1, 1:48	2. 0:17	2. —
3. Jesus preaches.	3. Tape 2, 1:30	3. 0:27	3. —
4. Jesus teaches.	4. Tape 2, 0:10	4. 0:37	4. 0:12
5. Jesus heals.	5. Tape 2, 0:02	5. 0:21	5. 0:41
6. Jesus shows anger.	6. Tape 2, 1:52	6. 1:11	6. 0:38
7. The garden of Gethsemane	7. Tape 3, 0:52	7. 1:23	7. 0:59
8. The Crucifixion	8. Tape 3, 1:26	8. 1:42	8. 1:39
9. The Resurrection	9. Tape 3, 1:52	9. 1:50	9. 1:36

Jesus Christ, Superstar is an optional musical portrayal of the last week of Jesus' life.

Question 3: What did you think when Jesus took the goatskin of water and dumped it on a man? Is this appropriate for a Messiah to do?

Answer 3: Some people would say that it was inappropriate; but then, the Pharisees thought that most of Jesus' actions were inappropriate—healing on the sabbath; not going through the ceremonial cleansing before eating; eating with sinners and tax collectors; forgiving prostitutes; welcoming a Roman soldier; and helping a pagan woman and her daughter, to name a few.

Question 4: Jesus tells us that we should not be anxious about clothes and other material items. How does this influence you and your friends when you see all the material possessions advertised on TV or displayed at the mall?

Answer 4: Our culture is materially obsessed; a person is often judged by his car or her make-up and clothing. Brand labels on shoes and pants are in; generic labels are out. This is one more area in which being a Christian means that we will not follow the crowd.

Question 5: What do you think of Jesus' using the staff to illustrate his point about judging a neighbor in Matthew 7:1-3? Is humor appropriate for religious teachers? Can humor really be found in the Bible?

Answer 5: Humor is definitely found in the Gospels. Most scholars believe that Jesus' teachings "Why do you see the speck in your neighbor's eye, but do not notice the log in your own eye?" (Matthew 7:3); "It is easier for a camel to go through the eye of a needle than for someone who is rich to enter the kingdom of God" (Matthew 19:24); and his nicknaming James and John "Sons of Thunder" (Mark 3:17) are all examples of Jesus' using humor to make a point.

SESSION 3: *JESUS OF NAZARETH— CHRIST THE MASTER STORYTELLER*

Franco Zeffirelli has taken the parable of the prodigal son and placed it in a different setting, just as the Gospel writers did in their own differing versions of Jesus' words and actions. As your group takes a closer look at this familiar parable about the nature of God, watch carefully how Jesus uses the power of storytelling to overcome the enmity between Peter and Matthew.

View the segment where Jesus enters Matthew's house and, seeing Peter and the others looking through the doorway, tells the parable of the prodigal son. When Peter and Matthew understand that Jesus intends for it to apply to them, they embrace (Tape 2, Start–0:16).

DISCUSSING & LEARNING

Have a youth read aloud the parable of the prodigal son (Luke 15:1-2 and 15:11-32). Have the group compare the setting of the parable in Luke with that in the movie.

Question 1: How is new meaning expressed in the film version of this parable?

Have a youth read aloud Luke 15:3-7 and Matthew 18:10-14—two versions of the parable of the lost sheep set in different ways to emphasize different aspects of its meaning.

Question 2: Why does Peter hate Matthew so much?

Answer 2: Because Peter is a loyal Jew and Matthew is collaborating with the Romans so that he may hold the lucrative position of tax collector. Note that in Luke 15:1, "tax collectors and sinners" are lumped together.

Question 3: With whom do Peter and Matthew identify in Jesus' story?

Answer 3: Peter identifies with the elder son; Matthew identifies with the prodigal son.

Question 4: What happens to the disciples as they hear this parable is what should happen to us also. If the Scriptures are to become God's Word to us (not just a collection of old stories), we need to see ourselves in Jesus' teachings. Do you see yourself in either of the characters?

Question 5: What are the stories—biblical, literary, or even family—that have affected your life?

SESSION 4: JESUS—A POWERFUL AND ANGRY JESUS

The film *Jesus* is based solely on Luke's Gospel, with an occasional scene added to enhance the meaning of the Scripture. In the following scenes we see that there is a toughness beneath Jesus' gentleness, especially when he confronts injustice and hypocrisy. One added scene shows the chief priests meeting with Governor Pilate, who warns them that if they allow Jesus to disturb the peace, he will hold them accountable. This adds a political motive to Jesus' enemies' plans to get rid of him.

DISCUSSING & LEARNING

View the segment that includes Palm Sunday (1:09) and Jesus' cleansing of the Temple (1:11).

Question 1: Why would Jesus choose a donkey to ride into Jerusalem?

Answer 1: The lowly donkey illustrates Jesus' humility and that he comes in peace. A warrior-messiah, which was what the crowds and many of his disciples wanted, would ride into Jerusalem on a horse.

© 1979 INSPIRATIONAL FILMS, INC.

Question 2: Why is Jesus so sad when he sees Jerusalem?

Answer 2: He knows that the people who cheer him will turn against him when they learn that he will not lead a revolt against Rome. And he can see that when they do revolt, they will not be able to win against their conquerors, who will destroy their city. (See Luke 19:41-44.)

Question 3: Were you surprised at the forcefulness of Jesus' actions in upsetting things at the Temple? Why was he so upset?

Answer 3: Jesus' reasons are only hinted at in his quotations from Isaiah and Jeremiah, but it might be that the money changers and animal handlers were cheating or charging outrageous prices. Then, too, they were using the outer court for their sales, the only place in the Temple where Gentiles were allowed to pray—and who could pray in that bedlam?

Question 4: How does the parable of the vineyard and the wicked tenants sum up the controversy between Jesus and the chief priests and Pharisees?

Answer 4: Jesus' enemies saw that the story was directed toward them. In the Jewish Scriptures, a vineyard often stood for Israel. The owner of the vineyard was God, who had sent prophets in the past, many of whom had been persecuted. Now God has sent Jesus; and when the wicked tenants kill him, they will be punished by God. Nothing that Jesus says in these film scenes will set well with his enemies. Jesus is almost inviting his death.

When you have finished with all four films, have a youth read Mark 8:27-31 again. Discuss with the group how the films have helped them in developing their image of Christ.

FINDING THE FILMS

If you have trouble finding the Jesus movies at your local video rental store or Christian bookstore, contact the publishers below for these possibly hard-to-get films; or call the central ordering number 800-672-1789 (for those films listed with CEN).

The Gospel According to Matthew
The Visual Bible
800-673-1596 [Item 1889710008]
or 800-672-1789 [CEN 807685]

Jesus of Nazareth
Gateway Films/Value Video
800-523-0226 [Item 1137] or
800-672-1789 [CEN 475309]

Jesus
The Jesus Project
800-523-0226 or
800-672-1789 [CEN 475309]

Give 'Em the Silent Treatment

A wonderful contrast to the movies featured here would be Cecil B. DeMille's 1927 silent movie *King of Kings*. Most youth have never seen a silent film and will be fascinated by the ways it differs from what they are accustomed to. This would be especially effective for a Lenten study that emphasizes silence as a way of approaching God. Watch for the amazing "two-color Technicolor" resurrection! Yes, even in 1927 color was possible, but extraordinarily expensive as well. DeMille argued that color would enhance the power of the Resurrection. (And he was right!) Be aware that there was a 1961 remake of *King of Kings,* directed by Nicolas Ray. While this is an intriguing version of the life of Christ, it is not as impressive as the silent original.

The Hunchback of Notre Dame

A Topsy-Turvy Retreat

He wasn't some handsome king. Nothing about the way he looked made him attractive to us. He was hated and rejected; his life was filled with sorrow and terrible suffering. No one wanted to look at him. We despised him and said, "He is a nobody!" He suffered and endured great pain for us, but we thought his suffering was punishment from God.

Isaiah 53:2-4

PURPOSE Youth will learn to look at others and themselves through Christ's eyes—God's children are in all sizes, colors, and conditions.

BACKGROUND Walt Disney's *The Hunchback of Notre Dame* is 95 minutes long and is rated G. The music for the film is by Alan Menken, and the lyrics are by Stephen Schwartz.

CAUTIONS The themes may be more bleak than what many people expect of a G-rated Disney movie. Over its course, *The Hunchback* depicts a mother's death, cruelty, racial discrimination, and lust. Still, the movie is certainly a suitable one for adolescents. As always, be sure to preview the movie in order to familiarize yourself with its themes before using this program.

SYNOPSIS In his determination to rid Paris of the Gypsy community, Judge Claude Frollo is responsible for the death of a young mother. As his penance, Frollo is forced to "care" for her misshapened infant son. Frollo hides the child he names Quasimodo—a name meaning "half formed"—in the belltower of the

Topsy-Turvy Activities

The Topsy-Turvy Festival!

Encourage the group to come in colorful, mixed-up clothing worn backward. (Some enterprising group members may even find a way to wear clothing upside down.) Greet each person at the door, saying, "Goodbye! See you soon!" Let the meeting progress (or regress) that way—dessert at the beginning of the meeting (upside-down cake, of course); backward relay races; a game of Charades with film titles acted out backward (example: Dame Notre of Hunchback The); a game of Twenty Questions, where the person giving the answers must say yes when he or she means no and vice versa. If it is someone's birthday, wish him or her "a very merry unbirthday" and wish each of the others happy birthday. End the event by putting on nametags and introducing visitors. Use your imagination and the imaginations of your group members.

Barriers

Call a public or private rehabilitation agency in your area and invite a

Cathedral of Notre Dame. He tells Quasimodo that he is so hideous and different from the people of the outside world that he will suffer only ridicule if he ever ventures out. Encouraged by his conversations with three stone gargoyles (his only companions), Quasimodo sneaks out of the cathedral for the "Feast of Fools" and is crowned "King of the Fools." The crowd begins to ridicule him; however, the Gypsy dancer Esmeralda rescues him. Misunderstanding her kindness for something more, Quasimodo becomes smitten with her—as do Frollo and the Captain of the Guard, Phoebus. Frollo's obsession with Esmeralda leads him to decide that he will have her for his own or kill her. Chases and battles ensue, resulting in Frollo's defeat, Esmeralda in the arms of the heroic Phoebus, and the equally heroic Quasimodo as the toast of the city.

BEFORE THE SESSION

Recruit adult helpers. Try to recruit one adult for every eight youth. Give these helpers specific instructions (or written guidelines). You may want to have a meeting before the retreat to discuss guidelines and expectations and to help ease volunteers' anxieties.

Room setup is essential. Some games require movable sturdy chairs, and others require lots of room. Decide where small groups will meet.

USING THESE SESSIONS & ACTIVITIES

These three retreat sessions and activities could be adapted to fit a number of formats—besides, of course, a retreat—including an intergenerational format involving all age groups. All the formats require viewing Walt Disney's *The Hunchback of Notre Dame* in its entirety before the discussion or activity. Therefore, using a one-session format would require a lengthy time slot or viewing the film at an earlier time. Several sessions are suggested if you use this program in other than a retreat format.

Other excellent and slightly different film versions of the Hunchback story are available, so one or more alternative versions could be viewed as well. However, the discussion questions for these sessions center around issues raised by the lyrics from the Disney film and its songs—so listening to the songs while viewing the video or listening to them on the soundtrack recording will be necessary.

MATERIALS

- Walt Disney's *The Hunchback of Notre Dame* video
- TV and VCR
- Optional: Walt Disney's *The Hunchback of Notre Dame* soundtrack
- Optional: versions of the movie on video (see page 59)
- Optional: The novel *The Hunchback of Notre Dame,* by Victor Hugo
- Optional: Blindfolds, earplugs, set of crutches, and a wheelchair
- Optional: Internet access

VIDEO VIEWING Begin with an opening prayer. View *The Hunchback of Notre Dame.* When viewing clips, use the Video Viewing chart below.

Suggestion: Preview the film on the VCR that you will use with the retreat. Make note of these key scenes so you can fast forward during the retreat, using these approximate start-end times and your VCR counter.

Start-End	Event	Count
0:00–0:07	"The Bells of Notre Dame"	_____
0:12–0:17	"Out There"	_____
0:21–0:26	"Topsy-Turvy"	_____
0:36–0:39	"God Help the Outcasts"	_____
0:46–0:48	"Sanctuary"	_____
0:48–0:51	"Hellfire"	_____
0:56–0:59	"A Guy Like You"	_____
1:08–1:10	"The Court of Miracles"	_____
Closing Credits	"Someday"	_____

---

representative to visit, bringing a client or two along. These persons could tell your group what it is like to have physical disabilities in your community, including issues such as handicap accessibility and acceptance by others. Many agencies have educational programs just for youth.

A related activity would be to set up simulation exercises to experience firsthand the barriers disabled individuals face daily. The group

may go to the mall and take a wheelchair to try to get in and out of stores or get a drink of water. Have the "able-bodied" youth and the "disabled" youth notice others' reactions. (Do people stare or sneak a peek? Do people speak differently?) See how much more difficult it is to travel, communicate, and experience all of life while using crutches, wearing earplugs, or wearing a blindfold. Be sure to have plenty of adult supervision and

allow discussion time. A person or persons with physical disabilities could lead this exercise.

Sanctuary

Use the Internet or a trip to the local library to learn more about the Sanctuary Movement in the United States. Your library's computers or periodical literature guides should cover the last 10 to 15 years, when this issue has been in the news off and on.

SESSION 1: WHO IS THIS HUNCHBACK?

DISCUSSING & LEARNING

During the retreat, or if your format allows it, view all three alternative versions. You will be able to use the following Discussing & Learning section. If your format allows you to view only one alternative, make it the 1939 Charles Laughton version. The Disney artists clearly drew inspiration from this version for their set designs and similar willingness to change the book's ending.

Question 1: Name some differences between the Disney version of the Hunchback's story and the 1939 version.

Answer 1: In the 1939 version

a) Quasimodo is unable to hear, save for the sound of the bells;
b) Phoebus is murdered by Frollo— the crime for which Esmeralda is imprisoned;
c) Esmeralda marries a poet named Gringoire, with whom she lives happily ever after;
d) any explanation of how Quasimodo came to live in the Notre Dame Cathedral is absent.

Question 2: Consider these alterations by both the 1939 and Disney versions of the 1831 novel by Victor Hugo. In the novel

a) Phoebus never loved Esmeralda;
b) Phoebus led Esmeralda on, although he was engaged to and then married another woman;
c) Esmeralda died by hanging, and it was Phoebus who carried out the sentence;
d) Frollo was not a judge but an evil priest of the cathedral;
e) Quasimodo disappeared after Esmeralda's death, and years later his bones were discovered lying next to hers in the crypt.

Have a youth read the touching ending to Victor Hugo's novel to the group. Why do you suppose the filmmakers have made changes to a classic story? What would have happened if no changes had been made? Do you think that it is appropriate for drastic changes to be made to a story without the permission of the author?

Answer 2: Possibilities are fear of criticism; concern about popular appeal; and, most importantly, box office receipts.

> About a year and a half or two years after the events with which this history concludes, when a search was made in the vault of Montfaucon for the body of Oliver le Daim, who had been hung two days previously, and to whom Charles VII had granted the favour to be interred in better company at Saint-Laurent, among these hideous carcasses were found two skeletons in a singular posture. One of these skeletons, which was that of a woman, had still upon it the fragments of a dress that had once been white; and about the neck was a necklace of the seeds of adrezarach, and a little silk bag braided with green beads which was open and empty. These things had been of so little value that the hangman no doubt had not thought it worth his while to take them. The other, by which this first was closely embraced, was the skeleton of a man. It was remarked that the spine was crooked, the head depressed between the shoulders, and one leg shorter than the other. There was, however, no rupture of the vertebrae of the neck, and it was evident that the person to whom it belonged had not been hanged. He must have come hither and died in the place. When those who found this skeleton attempted to disengage it from that which it held in its grasp, it crumbled to dust.
>
> The conclusion of *Notre Dame de Paris* (*The Hunchback of Notre Dame*) by Victor Hugo (1831)

Here is a brief history of the Sanctuary Movement: Refugees from Latin American military dictatorships came to America, seeking protection; but the US government would not grant political asylum to refugees from governments it supported. Some churches and church leaders responded to this plight, risking civil disobedience by providing shelter or a place to hide in the church. You may even be able to locate a guest speaker who has experienced first-hand the ancient idea of sanctuary. A book that would be helpful is *Sanctuary: A Resource Guide for Understanding and Participating in the Central American Refugees' Struggle* (1985), Gary MacEoin, Editor (ISBN 0-06-065372-8). Doing an Internet search will provide a wealth of information. Always pre-search so that you can guide your group to the most useful articles as you find them.

Chants

The chants of the medieval church have experienced a recent surge in popularity in secular culture. In addition to listening to the sections of *The Hunchback* soundtrack that feature these chants, listen to one of the bestselling collections of Gregorian chants. Invite a musician or your music director to teach the group to chant.

SESSION 2: FOOLISH CHRISTIANS!

THEME The love of Jesus has the power to turn our world gloriously upside down.

> He was given the book of Isaiah the prophet. He opened it and read, "The Lord's Spirit has come to me, because he has chosen me to tell the good news to the poor. The Lord has sent me to announce freedom for prisoners, to give sight to the blind, to free everyone who suffers, and to say, 'This is the year that the Lord has chosen.'" Jesus closed the book, then handed it back to the man in charge and sat down. Everyone in the meeting place looked straight at Jesus. Then Jesus said to them, "What you have just heard me read has come true today."
>
> Luke 4:17-21

DISCUSSING & LEARNING
Listen to or "view" the songs "Topsy-Turvy" and "The Court of Miracles."

Question 1: What is the purpose of Topsy-Turvy Day? Did it succeed?

Answer 1: Topsy-Turvy Day (based on the ancient Feast of Fools) was intended to honor what is low and despised in the world. Ugliness is celebrated, for example; and the poor and downtrodden are lifted to positions of power and esteem. Unfortunately, the human failings of the crowd occasionally caused them to forget their purpose and return to their everyday behaviors; for example, Quasimodo is crowned king and then ridiculed.

Question 2: The Feast of Fools was held on "the sixth of January." Why is that date significant to Christians, and what is the link?

Answer 2: January 6 is the 12th day of Christmas—the day of Epiphany—a part of which is the celebration of Jesus' presentation at the Temple. The priest Simeon blessed Jesus and told Mary, "This child of yours will cause many people in Israel to fall and others to stand. The child will be like a warning sign" (Luke 2:34). Have a youth read the Scripture. In what ways does Jesus cause people to stand?

Question 3: The "Court of Miracles" is "where the lame can walk and the blind can see." What is meant by that?

Answer 3: The Court of Miracles, the hang-out for the despised and outcast of the city, is a community in which people can find approval and acceptance of who they are—disabilities and all. Because these persons did not find much of society to be accepting, it was a miracle to be in a place that was.

SESSION 3: GREAT GARGOYLES!

THEME God does not view us by our earthly, materialistic standards. With Christ we are wise, acceptable, and holy.

> My dear friends, remember what you were when God chose you. The people of this world didn't think that many of you were wise. Only a few of you were in places of power, and not many of you came from important families. But God chose the foolish things of this world to put the wise to shame. He chose the weak things of this world to put the powerful to shame. What the world thinks is worthless, useless, and nothing at all is what God has used to destroy what the world considers important. God did all this to keep anyone from bragging to him. You are God's children. He sent Christ Jesus to save us and make us wise, acceptable, and holy.
>
> 1 Corinthians 1:26-30

DISCUSSING & LEARNING
Listen to or "view" the songs "Out There" and "A Guy Like You."

The first three of the following questions can lead to an important

---

Outcast
Send one member of the group (choose a good sport) on a short errand. While he or she is gone, instruct the rest of the group to ignore him or her when he or she returns. Then lead the group in a game or relay that the errand runner, upon returning, will be unable to join. After the game, discuss with the errand runner how it felt to be an outcast. Let others tell of their experiences when they didn't fit in. This may lead to a discussion of how misfits, visitors, or new members might be more quickly included in the life of the group.

Renaissance Festival
Visit a Renaissance festival in your area. These events (usually over a period of several consecutive weekends, once a year) are excellent opportunities to experience a medieval street festival with some of the games, foods, street performers, and other events that took place in Europe during the Middle Ages.

Sanctuary Game
Convert an old standby game to the theme of the movie. For instance, give directions to a secluded place on the church or retreat center grounds where the evening devotions will be held. This is "sanctuary." Announce that guards are prowling the area

discussion about self-image. Putting oneself into each of these characters' places is essential to help the youth identify the different types of behaviors and feelings related to this issue. Most youth can relate to feelings of insecurity and inferiority similar to those that Quasimodo feels. Significant is whether the youth intend to follow the gargoyles' model, resulting in respect and encouragement, rather than Frollo's model of ridicule and put-downs.

Question 1: Are there times when you have felt like Quasimodo? (Like you didn't fit in a particular group? Like your appearance would be ridiculed if you ventured out?) What was the effect of these feelings on your behavior?

Answer 1: (personal opinion)

Question 2: Have there been times when you behaved like Frollo (criticized the appearance and character of another for selfish or cruel reasons, such as envy or fear of your own embarrassment)? How did you feel afterward?

Answer 2: (personal opinion)

Question 3: Are there times when you have behaved like the gargoyles: Hugo, Victor, and Laverne (tried to bolster another person's damaged self-concept by pointing out that person's assets and strong qualities)? How did you feel afterward? Can you identify the Hugos, Victors, and Lavernes in your life? Who makes you feel good about yourself?

Answer 3: (personal opinion)

Question 4: Quasimodo says that people "out there . . . all live unaware . . . heedless of the gift it is to be them." What are some things you can do to appreciate life more fully or "treasure ev'ry instant"?

Answer 4: One exercise that will help your youth think about this question in more concrete terms is to give them each a small box of raisins to eat, but only allow them to eat one raisin per minute—as a way of savoring each morsel. Leading the group in a learning activity (such as the disability sensitivity event, described in Topsy-Turvy Activities) can help stimulate appreciation for things many take for granted.

SESSION 4: SANCTUARY!

THEME God provides safety and comfort—sanctuary—for those who seek them.

> I come to you, LORD, for protection. Don't let me be ashamed. Do as you have promised and rescue me. Listen to my prayer and hurry to save me. Be my mighty rock and the fortress where I am safe. You, LORD God, are my mighty rock and my fortress. Lead me and guide me, so that your name will be honored. Protect me from hidden traps and keep me safe. You are faithful, and I trust you because you rescued me.
>
> **Psalm 31:1-5**

and will be arresting anyone attempting to get to the sanctuary. Select a few mature youth and adults as the guards, giving them a few minutes to devise a strategy and to position themselves before you release the youth to make their way to "sanctuary." If the guards capture anyone, have them "interrogate" the prisoner briefly and then let him or her go so that everyone will be able to make it to devotions on time.

Topsy-Turvy Parade
The street performers were instrumental in Topsy-Turvy Day. Plan a Topsy-Turvy Parade. Some of your youth may have street-performing skills such as juggling, baton twirling, gymnastics, cheerleading, or mime. Have them prepare to perform in the festival or parade. This would be an excellent opportunity to introduce the youth to a basic purpose of clown ministry—to turn "my sorrow into joyful dancing" (Psalm 30:11). Teach them five- to ten-second skits or activities that can be done on a parade route. These skits should emphasize the uplifting of the mundane, the commonplace, and the powerless. Some examples:

- A youth wears a sign that says "free kisses"; but when the parade watcher is approached by the "fool," the fool feigns bashfulness and hands him or her a candy kiss instead of a real one.

DISCUSSING & LEARNING

Listen to or "view" the songs "God Help the Outcasts," "Sanctuary," and "Someday."

Question 1: Esmeralda sings, "Were you an outcast, too?" Can you think of parallels between Quasimodo's and Esmeralda's depiction in the movie and the portrait of Jesus in the Bible?

Answer 1: Point out that Quasimodo is celebrated as the King of Fools, only to have the crowd turn on him. Jesus was celebrated as he rode into Jerusalem; but by the week's end, the crowd had turned on him, mocking him with a crown of thorns and the label "King of the Jews" as he was crucified. Jesus' place of upbringing (Nazareth) and career (carpenter) were sources for ridicule; Esmeralda's place of upbringing and way of life are ridiculed. Jesus chose to spend time and commune with the outcast, downtrodden, and despised of his day. Your youth will think of many other examples.

Question 2: What does it mean when Quasi stands in the tower of Notre Dame, holds Esmeralda above his head, and cries, "Sanctuary! Sanctuary!"?

Answer 2: There is an ancient understanding of the sacred character of holy places. In the Israel of the Old Testament, certain cities were designated as places of refuge and protection (see Deuteronomy 19:1-13). By the Middle Ages (when *Hunchback* takes place), every church was considered a place of protection—a sanctuary. Civil law was not in effect on the church grounds. The idea of diplomatic embassies, providing political asylum for persons seeking to defect, comes out of this history.

Question 3: Read Jesus' parable of the Pharisee and the tax collector (Luke 18:9-14). What parallels do you see between this parable and Esmeralda's words in "God Help the Outcasts"? What is Esmeralda teaching us about prayer?

Answer 3: In her prayer, Esmeralda approaches God, humbly asking for nothing for herself but only for others. Meanwhile, self-concerned parishioners are praying for wealth, glory, and fame. In the parable, Jesus says that the prayer that is blessed is the humble one offered by the tax collector (a disrespected outcast as well). Be sure to listen to Frollo's prayer in "Hellfire" as another example of how not to pray. Praying for "things" such as wealth and success can lead to problems; such prayers focus on the self and can lead to an attitude of conceit. It is always far better to pray for others and to remain open to the movement of God's will in your own life.

Question 4: Do you believe that "Someday we may yet live and let live"? And how about, "Someday life will be fairer, Need will be rarer, Greed will not pay"?

Answer 4: (personal opinion, but let's hope so!)

- An inexpensive feather duster is used to gently tickle someone under the chin. A feather is plucked from the duster and left with the parade watcher as a reminder to smile.
- Use a rubber stamp and an ink pad (washable ink, of course) to stamp the hand of the parade watcher with a cute or friendly stamp.
- Use a key to unlock the smile on the "fool's" face, then gently turn the key on the face of a parade watcher to unlock his or her smile as well.

These and other suggestions can be found in the excellent book *Clown Ministry*, by Floyd Shaffer (Group Books).

Take Your Show on the Road!

Get permission well in advance to bring your Topsy-Turvy Parade to a mall, a care center, a halfway house, a homeless shelter, a hospital, Sunday school classes, or even worship! Have someone be prepared to explain "Topsy-Turvy Theology" to the people you visit. Make sure that everybody dresses up in the "topsy-turvy" outfits or something equally ridiculous. Friendly masks are allowed, but scary or horrible ones are not.

© 1962 UNIVERSAL PICTURES COMPANY, INC.

We Are Precious in His Sight: A Racism Retreat

Though Jesus commanded us to love one another, we know that we have a hard enough time just loving ourselves. How can we love people who are different from us in manner, convention, and appearance? The world says no—it is not possible, but . . .

But now that faith has come, we are no longer subject to a disciplinarian, for in Christ Jesus you are all children of God through faith. As many of you as were baptized into Christ have clothed yourselves with Christ. There is no longer Jew or Greek, there is no longer slave or free, there is no longer male and female; for all of you are one in Christ Jesus. And if you belong to Christ, then you are Abraham's offspring, heirs according to the promise.

Galatians 3:25-29

Therefore lift your drooping hands and strengthen your weak knees, and make straight paths for your feet, so that what is lame may not be put out of joint, but rather be healed.

Pursue peace with everyone, and the holiness without which no one will see the Lord. See to it that no one fails to obtain the grace of God; that no root of bitterness springs up and causes trouble.

Hebrews 12:12-15a

"There's a lot of ugly things in the world, Son. I wish I could keep them all away from you. That is never possible."

—Atticus Finch to son, Jem, in
To Kill a Mockingbird

VIDEO VIEWING
We recommend viewing each movie in its entirety. Below are the key scenes from the three primary films for the retreat. The key scenes and times for the optional movies are listed within the respective sessions.

Suggestion: Preview the film on the VCR that you will use with the program. Make note of these key scenes so you can fast forward during the program, using these approximate start-end times and your VCR counter.

ENEMY MINE

Start-End	Event	Count
0:16–0:25	Davidge escapes from the Drak; he doesn't kill him.	_____
0:31–0:33	Jerry saves Davidge's life.	_____
0:35–0:38	Jerry and Davidge apologize for making disparaging comments about each other's religious figures.	_____
0:41–0:43	Jerry and Davidge fight.	_____
0:44–0:46	Jerry cries when Davidge leaves.	_____
0:56–1:03	Jerry tells his lineage and asks Davidge about his.	_____
1:03–1:10	Jerry dies, and Davidge delivers the baby Drak.	_____
1:32–1:42	Davidge defends Drak slaves and saves Zameese.	_____

A FAMILY THING

Start-End	Event	Count
0:11–0:15	Earl reads to his father the letter from his mother.	_____
0:23–0:29	Earl finds his brother, and they talk over coffee.	_____
0:30–0:31	Earl gets mugged and car-jacked.	_____
0:36–0:38	Virgil comes home and finds Earl on the couch.	_____
0:44–0:47	Aunt Tee introduces Earl as her nephew.	_____
0:50–0:53	Aunt Tee speaks to Ray and Virgil. Earl leaves.	_____
0:53–0:56	Ray and Earl have a fist fight.	_____
0:57–1:00	Earl tries to connect with a family in a restaurant.	_____
1:06–1:07	Earl apologizes to Ray.	_____
1:10–1:17	Ray shares his bedroom with Earl.	_____
1:19–1:25	Earl talks with Virgil.	_____
1:28–1:39	Aunt Tee gives Earl his mother's photo and tells the story of the day he was born (some nudity).	_____
1:41–End	Ray goes back to Arkansas with Earl.	_____

TO KILL A MOCKINGBIRD

Start-End	Event	Count
0:15–0:17	Atticus is asked to defend Tom.	_____
0:19–0:21	Scout, Jem, and Dell spy on the courtroom.	_____
0:21–0:22	Hewell confronts Atticus.	_____
0:38–0:40	Atticus explains seeing from another point of view.	_____
0:43–0:47	Drunken Hewell scares Jem.	_____
1:00–1:05	Atticus and family face a mob at the jailhouse.	_____
1:06–1:41	Tom's trial takes place.	_____
1:30–1:37	Atticus gives closing arguments.	_____
1:43–1:46	Atticus reacts to the news of Tom's death.	_____
1:47–1:50	Drunken Hewell appears at the Robinsons' when Atticus breaks the news to Helen.	_____

THEME
Racism, bigotry, and prejudice create barriers between individuals and groups of people. Grace breaks down those barriers, allowing diversity to exist without bigotry. Through the grace of God, people can accept one another as they are—brothers and sisters, children of the same family.

PURPOSE
Youth will learn to tell the difference between prejudice, bigotry, and racism and will begin to cope with their personal prejudices as well as those of family and friends. Lessons learned will help youth fight racism in our society.

MATERIALS
- Videos: *Enemy Mine, A Family Thing, To Kill a Mockingbird;* Optional: *Four Little Girls* (HBO documentary), *The Milagro Beanfield War*
- TV and VCR
- Flip chart and markers
- Paper, pencils, masking tape, small candies such as M&Ms®, small sandwich bags with twist ties, chocolate statue such as an Easter Bunny

USING THESE SESSIONS & ACTIVITIES

This can be a weekend retreat beginning with Friday dinner and ending with lunch on Sunday. (Or with adaptation, this can be a 3- or 4-day camp or a series of evening youth events.) The format of the retreat is a series of consciousness-raising movies and brainstorming sessions designed to help youth 1) become aware of their own prejudices, and 2) explore ways youth can personally break down racial barriers in their families and peer groups. The movies were chosen to illustrate not only personal prejudice and racism, but also how individuals and groups may overcome such things.

SESSION 1: RETREAT ICEBREAKER

Friday night after dinner and chores, meet in a large room with plenty of floor space. Open the session with prayer, and watch *Enemy Mine*.

BACKGROUND

Enemy Mine (1985) is 108 minutes long and is rated PG-13.

CAUTIONS

Enemy Mine is about cultural racism and is rated PG-13 for some profanity, gore, and violence.

SYNOPSIS

When they crash land on the same planet after a fearsome battle, a Drak and a human are forced to depend on each other to survive.

WHAT RACISM IS *NOT*

PREJUDICE: either positive or negative prejudgment on insufficient grounds

BIGOTRY: a more intense form of prejudice which carries the negative side of prejudgment

STEREOTYPING: attributing characteristics to a group simplistically and uncritically, and assuming that those characteristics are rooted in significant and essential differences

DISCRIMINATION: the act or practice of according differential treatment to persons on the basis of group, class, or category such as race, religion, gender

SCAPEGOATING: the act or practice of assigning blame or failure to persons or groups in place of other persons or groups to whom blame or failure actually belongs

By Robert Terry
Women's Theological Center, P.O. Box 1200, Boston, MA 02116

SESSION 2: "I'M NOT PREJUDICED; ONE OF MY BEST FRIENDS IS A DRAK."

Take a brief break. After the break, divide the larger group into smaller groups of six to twelve persons.

Say: "Many of our prejudices are learned at home or absorbed from the surrounding culture. We have been 'taught' to be bigoted against certain groups of people, not necessarily against individuals, but against whole groups or races."

Begin a discussion within each small group, encouraging participants to candidly discuss the prejudices they have been taught—their own "cultural racism" and prejudices against the following:

African Americans
Asian Americans
Native Americans
Caucasians
Asian Indians
Recent immigrants
Welfare mothers
Hispanics
Protestants
Catholics
Jews
Hindus
Islamics

Have each small group make a list of derogatory labels that cultural racism places on each of the above.

Say: "We learned each of these derogatory names from another person. Just as we acquired prejudice, we can learn to live in the ways God intends: in acceptance of each person as an individual, as a child of God, and as an equal to ourselves as a human being."

Ask someone to read aloud Galatians 3:25-29 and Hebrews 12:12-15a. Then instruct each small group to write a different ending for *Enemy Mine* that portrays a breakthrough in easing relations between humans and Draks (for example, a new title: *Enemies No More*). Have each of the small groups select a spokesperson to briefly summarize for the entire group their new ending. The whole youth group can have a vote to select the Academy Award®-winning finale. The Oscar® for the winning group can be a chocolate figure (or statue) of some kind.

DISCUSSING & LEARNING

Question 1: What attitudes or prejudices did the human, Davidge, exhibit concerning Draks in general? (Davidge thought that Draks were stupid, disgusting, dirty creatures, who were inferior to humans. His monologue at the beginning of the movie could describe the bigoted beliefs of any modern culture that exhibits hatred for another race.)

Question 2: What several things did Jerry do that enabled Davidge to change? (Jerry was able to share his religious beliefs with Davidge; he also showed acts of mercy.)

Question 3: How did Davidge's love for Zameese affect his feelings about Draks? (Davidge's feelings for Jerry's child turned him around completely. He realized Zameese was a lovable, loving sentient being.)

Question 4: After Davidge regained his health at the space station, how did his superiors and coworkers regard his new response to Zameese and the plight of the enslaved Draks? (They didn't understand. Because his views no longer matched theirs, they were suspicious of him.)

Question 5: Was Jerry or Davidge more accepting of the other first? (Jerry was first; it was not in the Drak species to be sarcastic or cruel.)

Question 6: Did Davidge always control his feelings about Draks? (No. He was verbal about how he felt but did not act on his feelings. He could not bring himself to kill Jerry when he had the chance.)

Question 7: What behavior of Davidge and Jerry parallels bigoted and racist feelings in the US? in other parts of the world? (Each character assumed that he knew the worst about the other and that he was superior to the other. This is also a fair assessment of the bigotry that exists in the former Yugoslavia, in France toward Algerians, in Germany toward the Turks, and in many other places across the globe.)

Question 8: How were indigenous people (Native Americans) treated by Europeans in the 1500's and 1600's? by people of non-indigenous descent today? (Indigenous peoples in both North and South America were treated as less than human. In Latin America, whole races were annihilated. Native Americans in the US have been forced to live on reservations. A form of enslavement exists today: Though Native Americans are supposedly welcome to leave the reservation to seek education and jobs, the prejudices against them as a people prohibit them from doing so.)

LEARNING ACTIVITY
Determine which scenes from *Enemy Mine* illustrate 1–5 below:

1. **Prejudice:** The reaction and response of Davidge's friends after his recovery shows how prejudice can affect how we view others.
2. **Bigotry:** Davidge's monologue about Draks at the beginning of the movie exemplifies bigotry.
3. **Stereotyping:** Davidge and Jerry's first reactions to each other are the reflection of hatred they had learned from their respective races.
4. **Discrimination:** Jerry's sense of superiority kept him from pitching in and helping Davidge build their shelter.
5. **Scapegoating:** Scapegoating is shown when Zameese is put in a cage to make an example to the other Draks, when the mining camp leaders cast blame onto others, when Davidge wanted to kill Jerry when he first saw him on the planet.

SESSION 3: WHAT'S RACISM, ANYWAY?
Saturday morning after breakfast, gather everyone into a room large enough to allow the youth to sit comfortably on the floor.

BEFORE THE SESSION
Use masking tape to mark off a 10-foot-by-10-foot square on the floor. Divide the small candies (or M&M® candies) into small bags. There should be 2 bags with 20 candies in each, 5 bags with 10 candies in each, and enough bags with 3 candies in each for everyone else in your group to receive one bag. (The number of bags will vary according to the size of the youth group. Make sure that there are at least three times as many bags with 3 candies as the combined number of bags with 10 or 20 candies.) Have extra candies on hand to share with the group after the activity.

LEARNING ACTIVITY
Open with prayer. Distribute a bag of candies to each youth. (Do not look at the bags to decide who will get the bags with more candies in them.) Tell the youth that they are not to eat the candy. Tell everyone who has a bag with 3 candies to stand within the bounds of the 10-foot-by-10-foot square on the floor. Tell the youth with the 20 and 10 candies that they may move freely around the room, that they are persons of power, that all the wealth in the room belongs to them. Tell those within the square that even though they constitute the majority within the room, they have no power and nothing belongs to them.

Explain the meaning of *apartheid,* which until recently was the accepted system in South Africa. Talk about facts and figures: 2 percent of the people had 97 percent of the land, power, and resources in South Africa. After Dutch colonization, the Afrikaner minority believed that oppression of the African majority population was essential for the white minority to retain power and their holdings.

Continue to expound on the evils of apartheid for quite a while. After a time (which the leader will observe and determine) the group within the square will become tired of standing in a confined space,

unable to move freely. Just before rebellion breaks out, allow everyone to sit wherever he or she wants to on the floor. Ask volunteers to tell how they felt during the activity.

After a discussion of their feelings, ask the participants again what they think true racism is. The youth should have a better understanding of how the actions of one group to suppress another define racism. Then let everyone eat the candies.

RACISM, BIGOTRY, PREJUDICE
Ask the group how they distinguish between prejudice and racism. Say: "Both hurt. Both wound and scar. The technical definition of *prejudice* is 'an unfavorable opinion or feeling formed beforehand without knowledge, thought, or reason.' *Prejudice* is something people carry in their minds. *Bigotry* is a more intense form of prejudice that carries the negative side of prejudgment. *Racism* is prejudice and bigotry put into practice."

(Adapted from "What Racism Is *Not*." See page 62.)

Continue: "Racism is different from racial prejudice and hatred. Racism involves having the power to carry out systematic discriminatory practices through both personal acts and through the major institutions of our society."

(Adapted from "What Curriculum Leaders Can Do About Racism," by Dr. Dalmo Della-Dora.)

Add: "Racism is the power to discriminate against and treat unjustly those who are different racially or ethnically. This unjust treatment is based on the belief in the innate superiority of one ethnic group over another. Racism is the translation of racist attitudes into action."

SESSION 4: IT'S A FAMILY THING
After a short break, open the session with prayer. Before beginning *A Family Thing*, ask the group if they remember the technical definition of *racism* from Session 3. Give the participants a reminder if needed.

After the movie, close with prayer. Then have lunch and free time (early Saturday afternoon).

BACKGROUND
A Family Thing (1995) is 109 minutes long and is rated PG-13.

CAUTIONS
This film contains profanity, racial slurs, and brief nudity (during a childbirth).

SYNOPSIS
Earl Pilcher reads a letter from his mother following her death and learns that she was not his biological mother. The letter tells Earl that he is not just of Scotch-Irish descent but is also of African descent. His biological mother was the Pilcher family domestic servant, who became pregnant through a forced relationship and rape by Earl's father. Earl travels to Chicago to locate his brother, Raymond, and meets a new set of relatives.

SESSION 5: "DADDY, WHO IS THAT WHITE MAN ON THE COUCH?"
Mid-Saturday afternoon, after snack time, assemble the group in a large room.

Open the session with prayer. Then discuss *A Family Thing*.

DISCUSSING & LEARNING
"You can't help how you was born and you can't help how you was raised."—Aunt Tee

"If you need help, don't call me; I'm through helping you."—Ray

"The good Lord love all the little babies the same."—Aunt Tee

Question 1: What did the news of Earl Pilcher's true heritage do to his sense of superiority and self-image? (He still felt superior but his self-image was destroyed.)

Question 2: Did Earl go find his brother for reasons other than his mother's request? (Probably curiosity and his need to know for sure; he was seeking verification.)

Question 3: Why did Ray pick up Earl at the hospital and take him home? (Ray felt sorry for him and knew he needed help and deep down, Ray was a good person.)

Question 4: Ray believes that he has good reason to be bitter. He lost his mother and was forced to move to a different part of the country. Is he right to blame his misfortune on Earl? Was Earl responsible for what happened to Ray? How do you explain his feelings? How much of Virgil's reaction to Earl was learned behavior from Ray? (Ray was not justified in blaming Earl for his misfortune, but he had spent his whole life convincing himself that he was. It was a very human response. His feelings were both human and racist. Only a small amount of Virgil's reaction was probably learned behavior. As an adult, Virgil was capable of making up his own mind and could have been different from his father. Instead, he chose to be as prejudiced, if not more so, than his father.)

Question 5: How does the response of Earl and Ray to each other reflect that of general society? (The reactions and responses of the two characters are pretty indicative of the general public. Only when individuals see each other as equals can attitudes of mistrust change.)

Question 6: Read Aunt Tee's statement about babies (see the beginning of this session). Were Aunt Tee's actions consistent with her beliefs? (Aunt Tee put her beliefs into practice. Even before she became blind, she seemed to see everyone in exactly the same light; rather than blaming others, she accepted the reality of her situation and learned how to live and love beyond it.)

Question 7: How did Earl express his diminished feeling of self-worth? (Earl, in his despair, used alcohol abuse and inappropriate behavior in the restaurant to express his frustrations and his lowered feeling of self-worth. He also made excuses for how he had acted his whole life.)

Question 8: Name the ways Ray says he has been "saved." Aunt Tee saved him in his adolescence, the Army saved him as a young adult, and his wife saved him from alcoholism. All three times he was saved from his own anger. How is the practical love of Christ reflected in Ray's life? (Ray becomes Earl's redeemer. Almost in spite of himself, Ray accepts Earl as a fellow human and as a part of his family.)

Question 9: Can we really command ourselves to love one another as Jesus and Aunt Tee did? (Yes, but it is extremely difficult.) What gets in the way? (Anger, hypocrisy, pride, prejudice, and jealousy prevent us from loving one another. These are the things that have to be dealt with before we can truly love and accept one another the way Christ accepts us.)

Question 10: How do you think Earl presented Ray to his family when the two brothers arrived at Earl's

house? (He might say: "Hey y'all, this is Ray, my brother.")

Question 11: What was Aunt Tee able to do to the "root of bitterness" present in the lives of Ray and Earl? (She got the brothers to acknowledge it by using their common denominator, their mother. This was the first step toward true reconciliation.)

Question 12: Did Aunt Tee love Earl? (Yes, unquestionably. He was family, he was a child of God, and he deserved love.)

SESSION 6: US VERSUS THEM

Saturday evening after dinner, play Us Versus Them, a youth group diversity indicator activity. Assemble the group in a large room with enough chairs for everyone. Open the session with prayer.

The leader will invite the youth to quickly pair up with someone whose first name starts with the same letter or whose last name starts with the same letter until everyone has a partner. Partners should sit in chairs, facing each other. Give each person a piece of paper and a pencil.

One person in each pair should write *Us* on the top of his or her paper; the other person should write *Them* on the top of his or her paper.

Then give everyone only 3 minutes to write down every word that he or she can think of that represents what is written on the top of his or her paper. Call time and instruct each pair to swap lists with another pair so that each has someone else's lists.

Allow approximately 3 minutes for the pairs to go through the new lists and to circle every item on the list that, in their opinion, falls under the category "Community." Call time and have each pair report to the entire group all the terms

they have circled. Discuss what the terms mean. (Expect the terms to reflect not only the cultural biases of the group but peer attitudes as well.)

Every pair of youth will have different terms listed under "Community." Explain to the group that every item on both lists should appear under the "Community" heading.

Ask a volunteer to write on the flip chart the group's suggestions for making the youth group more accepting and diverse. Save the sheets to take home and put up later in the youth meeting rooms in your church to remind the participants of the retreat.

SESSION 7: THE POWER SPECTRUM

Draw the Power Spectrum diagram (pages 66–67) ahead of time on large newsprint and tape it to a wall or window. Make a list of the types of persons who make up your community or use the list at the bottom of page 67. Make copies of the list for every two youth.

Have the youth think about the way they believe power is structured in the United States. Then have them work in pairs and use their beliefs to place the listed persons on the spectrum. Allow 10 to 15 minutes for the pairs to write the number on the spectrum next to each person.

Instruct the pairs to get together into groups of 4 or 6 (depending on the number of youth). Allow 20 minutes for the youth to discuss why they placed people where they did on the spectrum.

Reassemble the group. Ask for some discussion about who in the community has the most power and who has the least. Compare the power roles to other groups that the youth are members of— the band, sports teams, scouts, scholastic organizations, clubs, and others. In which groups does having power mean the most in order to succeed? What groups share the power equally among the members? What groups appreciate and celebrate diversity? What implications does this spectrum have for racism, classism, and social justice?

Close the session with a prayer that the power existing within the group not be used to put down others or to keep others from succeeding, thriving, growing, or feeling welcome. Invite everyone to start with the youth group in working toward diversity and acceptance of others for whoever they are.

SESSION 8: INSTITUTIONAL RACISM 101

BACKGROUND

To Kill a Mockingbird (1962) is 129 minutes long, in black and white, and is not rated.

CAUTIONS

To Kill a Mockingbird contains some violence (including shooting a rabid dog) and numerous racial slurs.

SYNOPSIS

To Kill a Mockingbird is set in depression-era Alabama; a sister and brother, Scout and Jem (and their friend Dell), do not remain unaffected when their father, Atticus Finch, takes on the defense of Tom Robinson, a black man accused of raping a white woman.

DISCUSSING & LEARNING

Question 1: Contrast the demeanor of the African American characters in To Kill a Mockingbird and A Family Thing. (In To Kill a Mockingbird, African Americans are passive on the surface and deferred to whites. In A Family Thing, African Americans demand to be treated as equals and are more assertive.)

Question 2: What similarities exist between the pre-'70s American South and the South African apartheid system? (keeping persons of color from thriving, maintaining the power system at the expense of a race, and fostering prejudice)

Question 3: What would you do if someone spit in your face? Why? (Possible answers are spit back, hit him or her, yell at him or her, do nothing. Most of us are completely caught off guard when confronted with inappropriate and violent behavior. As unpleasant as it might seem, every person should think ahead of time about what he or she might do in an extreme situation. Then he or she is more likely to do the right thing—turn the other cheek and forgive.)

Question 4: Evidence proved that Tom Robinson was innocent. On what basis do you think the jury found him guilty? (The decision was foregone. The accusation alone of a black man raping a white girl was considered proof. An all-white jury—a jury of the accusers' peers—could never pass a not-guilty verdict.)

Question 5: How did the Finch family relate to persons who worked for them? Who owed Atticus' law practice money? (They treated them with respect, as valued family members. Mr. Cunningham was indebted to Atticus Finch.)

Question 6: Scout recognized Mr. Cunningham on the jailhouse steps. What did she say that caused the lynch mob to leave? (Scout pointed out that Mr. Cunningham was indebted to her father and that she was a schoolmate of Mr. Cunningham's son. She put reality into perspective. Moreover, she shamed all those men, and defused the mob.)

Question 7: Why did Tom stop in the middle of his testimony after he told the jury he felt sorry for Mae Ella? (It was culturally unacceptable for a black person to pity a white person at that time.)

Question 8: Mr. Radley filled in the knot hole with cement and cut off Boo Radley's communication with Jem. How did the abuse and

POWER SPECTRUM

The Power Spectrum represents a theory of economic and social stratification often used by sociologists to help describe one way that power can be seen to operate in a community or in a nation.

1	2	3	4	5	6
These persons have no power or economic stability.		These persons generally operate on a bare minimum of power and economic stability.		These persons could be called the "Silent Majority." These and those at the bottom of the spectrum are the ones most affected by the policies and decisions made at higher levels of power.	

neglect that Boo Radley suffered as an individual parallel the abuse and neglect African Americans experienced in Macon County? (Both were alienated, mistrusted, and misunderstood. Truth about them was replaced with outrageous stories.)

Question 9: List the different ways Tom Robinson was dehumanized—treated as less than the person he was. (1. Everyone presumed his guilt because of his color. 2. No one considered him to be a man. 3. No one interviewed him prior to the trial.)

Question 10: How did Mr. Hewell manipulate the judicial system? (He used prejudice within the community to reinforce his lies.)

Question 11: Why did the members of the lynch mob feel threatened by Tom Robinson? (Because he was to be tried and have legal counsel, he represented a change in society. That change would have been more than the people in the community could bear, because it meant the end of their belief systems.)

Question 12: Why did the black preacher make Scout stand up when Atticus left the courtroom? (The preacher wanted Scout to join the African American community in their respect for her father.)

Question 13: Why did the sheriff choose to say that Hewell fell on his knife? (It wasn't true, but he also knew that Hewell was an evil person. He figured that Boo Radley would probably end up like Tom Robinson if the truth surfaced.)

Question 14: What sort of example did the Finch family set in Macon County, Alabama? (The Finch family acted in a just way. They were symbols of how society can be if individuals accept one another and act appropriately.)

Question 15: How did Atticus respond to the individuals who were the meanest and nastiest to him? (He turned the other cheek, and he was not intimidated by those who threatened him.)

Question 16: In what ways and situations did Atticus Finch exemplify Christlike behavior? (Atticus visited and helped the poor. He was the only person to visit Tom Robinson's family. He tried to do what was just. He understood justice and mercy and acted on it.)

Question 17: What was the moral basis for the prosecuting attorney's arguments? (There was no moral basis for the prosecuting attorney's arguments. The prosecutor used the racism in society as well as bigotry and fear to convict Tom Robinson.)

Have the group use the Power Spectrum to analyze the power structure of Macon County, assigning the *To Kill a Mockingbird* characters to different areas of the spectrum. The characters to be considered are the black preacher; members of the jury; Atticus Finch; Arthur "Boo" Radley; Mr. Cunningham; the sheriff; Tom Robinson; Jem, Scout, and their friends; Cal, the housekeeper; the people in the balcony, the people in the audience in the courtroom; other unseen residents of the town and county; the judge; members of the jury; prosecuting attorney.

OPTIONAL SESSION 9: THE MILAGRO BEANFIELD WAR

"I knew that Joe was destined to do something great."—Ruby Archuleta

The following sessions are optional due to their focus on an R-rated film. Base your use of the sessions on the maturity of your youth in dealing with the adult language and violence portrayed in *The Milagro Beanfield War*. As always, preview the entire movie and send home copies of the Student Movie Pass (the parent consent form on the inside back cover).

Open the session with prayer. Advise the group that this movie is intentionally full of symbolism.

7

These persons hold the line and help interpret for the rest of the community the policies and decisions made at higher levels of power.

8

9

These are the persons who often set the policies by which the nation and local communities operate. These are the persons who have the power to make the decisions that affect the life and structure of their communities.

10

Nurse
Doctor
Farmer
Engineer
Salesman
Mechanic
Bank Teller
Custodian
Lawyer
Truck Driver
Social Worker
Hospital Orderly
Police Officer
Welfare Parent
Clergy Person
Paid House Cleaner
Dish Washer

Bank President
Motel Worker
Local Merchant
Homeless Person
College Professor
Sanitation Worker
TV Executive
Factory Worker
School Teacher
Real Estate Agent
Migrant Farm
    Worker
Newspaper Editor
Fast-Food
    Employee
Owner of
    Newspaper

Owner of US
    Corporation
President of
    Chamber of
    Commerce
Chronically
    Unemployed
Insurance or Wall
    Street Broker
Elected Public
    Official
Civil Service
    Employee
CEO of US Corp.
Middle
    Manager

BACKGROUND

The Milagro Beanfield War (1988) is 118 minutes long and is rated R.

CAUTIONS

The Milagro Beanfield War is rated R for language and violence. However, the rating system of 1988 was apparently much stricter than that of nowadays. If this movie were to be released today, it would probably be rated PG (not even PG-13).

SYNOPSIS

A beanfield becomes the focus for a Hispanic American community in its efforts to stand up for its community and civil rights. A rich, powerful Anglo-American and a militia of strongmen try to stop the citizens of Milagro (*Milagro* means "miracle"), who have chosen not to let "progress" take over what has been theirs for 300 years.

VIDEO VIEWING

0:08–0:09—Joe tries to get a job with the development company and is brushed off.
0:15–0:18—When Joe kicks over an irrigation gate, flooding his father's old beanfield with water, he decides to ignore it and let the water come. In no time, the town is mobilized around the isolated incident.
0:23–0:24—Everyone watches Joe plow and work in the old field.
0:30–0:35—Bureaucrats go to work to stop Joe because he poses a threat to the development. A few individuals with money and power attempt to crush a whole powerless community.
0:44–0:46—The ghost causes the "miracle" of the newspapers.
0:46–0:52—At the town meeting, Charlie becomes the scapegoat.
1:16–1:18—Joe almost gives in to the buy-out; Ruby and his wife talk him out of it.
1:22–1:25—Amarante saves the beanfield and makes a personal sacrifice.
1:41–1:43—Shorty switches sides and saves Joe from Montana on the mountain.

OPTIONAL SESSION 10: INSTITUTIONAL RACISM 102

The agricultural irrigation present in each valley in the Sangre de Cristo mountains of New Mexico is one of the oldest continuous legal and physical systems in the US. Dating from the mid-1600's, irrigation law is quite complex. When Joe irrigated his miracle beanfield and completed a harvest, he reclaimed his family's agricultural land in spite of the Anglo's development plans.

Have someone read aloud Galatians 3:25-29 and Hebrews 12:12-15a.

DISCUSSING & LEARNING

Question 1: What purpose did the Coyote Ghost play in the movie? Who did he say he was? (The ghost says that he is Joe's father. He represents the holy spirit or the spirit of things good and wise.)

Question 2: In the governor's office, the group analyzed the Milagro community. They determined who were weakest and most vulnerable and how to neutralize them. Were their actions illegal? racist? (Yes, on both counts.) Were they following good business procedure? (The practices used by the developers and politicians in the governor's office are examples of the ends justifying the means. The tactics may be used, but they are far from good.)

Question 3: What did the development planning group decide they would not do to avoid charges of racism? Were their actions racist? Why or why not? (They chose to have Joe stopped without arresting him. If they had arrested Joe, activist/lawyer Charlie would publicize their actions as racist.)

Question 4: How were the police chief, forest rangers, and general store owner co-opted? (Each was promised some gain or fortune by the developers in return for helping

them to get the development off the ground.)

Question 5: Why was Charlie the lawyer made the first scapegoat by the development group? (Because he was an outsider and had a record, Charlie would easily lose credibility if he spoke out against the development.)

Question 6: What did Ruby say that convinced the lawyer to assist the town of Milagro? (She convinces him to go to the town meeting. When he does, she announces that he has come to speak.)

Question 7: As an outsider, how was Herbie initially treated? Why? (Herbie was treated pretty badly. These are examples of stereotyping by the community: Herbie was an outsider, a "gringo," a greedy Anglo geek looking to exploit them in some way, different.)

Question 8: Why did Joe have so many internal conflicts about the beanfield? How did Joe's wife feel about his beanfield project? (Growing the crop of beans was old-fashioned and not how Joe saw himself supporting his family. His wife seemed to reflect his feelings and conflicts. When he was up about the project, she was encouraging; when he was frustrated with the project, she wanted him to quit. Both seemed unsure of how it should go, but they never gave up.)

Question 9: What symbolism did Ruby understand about the beanfield before anyone but Joe, Amarante, and the ghost? (The beanfield represented life and the spirit of the community. The bean project had to be successful in order for the community to survive.)

Question 10: What do you think Shorty's decision to help Joe meant? Why did Shorty change his actions? (Shorty decided to do the right thing. He knew that he had not been acting properly toward the local people and he felt bad. The only way to redeem himself was to be the redeemer for the community.)

Question 11: Why didn't all the townspeople get behind the beanfield symbol from the start? What was their positive self-interest in the beans? (Fear keep the majority of the community from supporting the beanfield project. In the end they all realized that it meant their culture would survive.)

Question 12: Why and how were Charlie and Herbie accepted into the town structure even though they were Anglos? (As the people got to know them and realized they would not give up, they began to accept these two nonconformist outsiders. They both had gifts that were recognized by the community.)

Question 13: How was institutional racism portrayed in the movie? (Racism was disguised as development and presented as a good, healthy thing.)

Question 14: List the characters who exhibited Christlike behavior. How? (Ruby always saw good in others. Joe and his grandfather are unsuspecting redeemers. *Viejos* [the old men] are guardian angels.

Herbie and Charlie were both willing to make personal sacrifices. Shorty finally stood up and heard the call to do good.)

Have the group use the Power Spectrum to analyze the power structure of the town of Milagro, assigning the characters to different levels of the spectrum. The characters are Bernie, Devine, visible residents of the town, Charlie Bloom, Ruby, Amarante, the forest ranger, Montana, the governor, unseen residents of the town, the mayor, Herbie, Joe, Joe's wife, Devine's wife, Shorty, *los viejos* (the old man brigade), Joe's cow, the pig, the stone-throwing *vieja* (old woman).

OPTIONAL SESSION 11: FOUR LITTLE GIRLS
Watch the HBO documentary *Four Little Girls* to close the retreat. Discuss how things have changed since the church bombing in 1963. Plan a worship and Communion for the retreat end.

EPILOGUE FOR RACISM
Ask: Is it possible for people to truly change? Can a person really unlearn terrible things? (Yes, especially with Christ's help.)

Read the following excerpt from an editorial of a Southern newspaper:

"I was beaten here," John Lewis told 300 Selma churchgoers. "And now I stand here today as a U.S. Congressman." Nine-term Selma Mayor Joe Smitherman presented Lewis with the key to the city. "Back then, I called him an outside rabble-rouser," said Smitherman of Lewis. "Today, I call him one of the most courageous people I ever met."

"Back then" was March 8, 1965, when Lewis and other civil rights activists were beaten and bloodied by state police and sheriff's deputies on the Edmund Pettus Bridge. There, demonstrators tried, unsuccessfully that day, to start the March to Montgomery [Alabama]. The march to the capital was completed later that year. The march to racial enlightenment in American society continues.
(March 11, 1998—*The Columbus Ledger-Enquirer*, Columbus, Georgia)

Other resources and sources of additional material and videos:
- EPICA, 1470 Irving Street, NW, Washington, DC 20010, distributes textbooks and videos on racism and poverty in the Caribbean and Latin America.
- The Southern Poverty Law Center, Montgomery, Alabama, has produced an award-winning, nonsectarian series of studies for youth called *Teaching Tolerance*. The Southern Poverty Law Center monitors hate groups and crimes in the US.
- The NAACP—Call your local chapter.
- The Urban League—Call your local chapter.
- Other videos: *Mississippi Burning* (violent), *Gandhi* (violent), *From Montgomery to Mobile* (old documentary, but good), *Rosewood* (extremely violent)

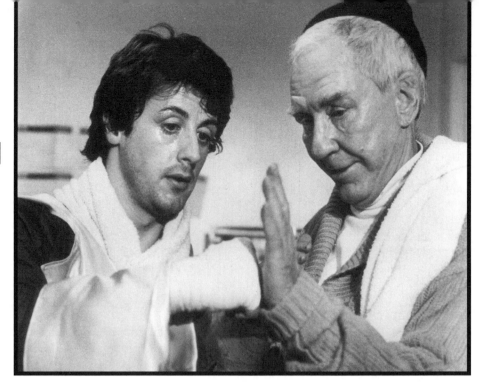

SPORTS MOVIE MARATHON

A Retreat Featuring
Rocky, Hoosiers, and *Rudy*

And now faith, hope, and love abide, these three; and the greatest of these is love.

1 Corinthians 13:13

THEME We find redemption, hope, and grace in our faithful relationship with Jesus Christ.

PURPOSE Within athletic competition, youth will learn valuable lessons that will prepare them for the game of life.

CAUTIONS All three movies, *Rocky, Hoosiers,* and *Rudy,* are rated PG. There are some spoken obscenities and some blood resulting from rough physical contact in the sports depicted. The principal characters in each of the films show some use of alcohol; only in *Hoosiers* is drinking clearly portrayed in a negative fashion. A sexual relationship between Rocky and his girlfriend is implied although not depicted. As always, leaders are encouraged to preview the films and send home a Student Movie Pass (parent consent form) prior to the event if you think that it is necessary.

MATERIALS
- *Rocky, Hoosiers,* and *Rudy* videos
- TV and VCR (If you have access to a portable projection TV, make arrangements to use it. A large-screen TV format can be a huge boost to the visibility and enthusiasm of action films.)
- Materials for the activities (one or both) listed on page 76
- Newsprint and markers

Each participant should bring
- Pen or pencil and a notebook
- Bible
- Sleeping bag or bed roll, sleeping clothes, toiletries, change of clothing, snacks, and everything else that goes with spending a night away on retreat

USING THESE SESSIONS & ACTIVITIES

This program is designed as a 24-hour retreat and bonding experience for boys ages 12 to 18 (but could easily be done with the whole youth group). This age range often extends over several levels of both physical and emotional maturity. Depending on the size of your group, you may want to limit participants to a narrower age range. However, widely variant ages is only one factor that can affect the success of a group-building retreat.

In the course of the retreat, the boys will be watching and discussing sports films that encourage growth in particular attitudes and issues of character. They will participate in games and activities that can draw the members closer together by helping them understand themselves more completely, their developing bodies and personalities, their relationships with others, and their relationship with God. The degree to which this goal can be achieved depends, in part, on the level of mutual respect, the willingness to explore feelings, the sense of safety present, and the degree to which cliques have been eliminated. Sensitivity to the dynamics of your group will guide you toward understanding what results you might expect.

It is possible, and highly recommended, to adapt this retreat into an experience for similarly aged youth and their fathers, guardians, or church mentors (perhaps a Father's Day lock-in). Have the adults participate in the activities and discussions along with the boys.

SUGGESTIONS FOR THE RETREAT

One of the great things about a retreat is getting away from familiar territory to focus on one topic and to participate intensively. If your group can afford to go to a campsite or hotel for this event, great! If you have facilities and ability to prepare meals, even better!

Having some open space for recreation is important. If you decide to have the retreat at your church, try to steer clear of the sanctuary or other areas that are regularly used by the group. New environs help people look at things in new ways rather than feel comfortable with the old. Be sure that there are enough male adult leaders participating to help with small-group discussion.

VIDEO VIEWING
Begin with an opening prayer. Then view the three movies where recommended in the program. If you've decided to view clips, use the Video Viewing chart.

Suggestion: Preview the films on the VCR that you will use with the program. Make note of these key scenes so you can fast forward during the program, using these approximate start-end times (hour:minutes) and your VCR counter.

ROCKY

Start-End	Event	Count
0:10–0:12	Rocky in pet store; our first view of Adrian	_____
0:12–0:15	Rocky collects money; meets with his loan shark boss.	_____
0:18–0:20	Mickey tells Rocky why he should give up boxing.	_____
0:26–0:28	Rocky counsels neighborhood girl.	_____
0:39–0:46	Rocky's first date with Adrian	_____
1:04–1:10	Mickey and Rocky argue; Rocky agrees to let Mickey manage him.	_____
1:19–1:23	Rocky's training sequence	_____
1:40–1:55	The main event	_____

HOOSIERS

Start-End	Event	Count
0:09–0:11	Townsfolk first meet with Norman.	_____
0:11–0:18	Norman's first basketball practice	_____
0:20–0:21	Norman talks with Jimmy about his gift; tells him that it is his choice.	_____
0:26–0:32	First game; only four men playing by game's end	_____
0:39–0:46	Norman's conversation with teacher	_____
0:38–0:40	Norman gets himself thrown out of game, so Shooter must coach.	_____
1:04–1:07	State championship final game	_____
1:43–1:53	The main event	_____

RUDY

Start-End	Event	Count
0:09–0:11	Rudy in class, then rejected to take bus trip to Notre Dame	_____
0:13–0:15	With Pete: "Having dreams is what makes life tolerable."	_____
0:21–0:24	Father tells story of his father's failed farm.	_____
1:02–1:04	Priest tells Rudy, "The answers come in God's time."	_____
1:28–1:35	Rudy doesn't make dress list for final game; quits.	_____
1:39–1:50	The last game	_____

DISCUSSING & LEARNING

Question 1: Rocky is a good and kind man, yet he lacks direction. What are some times that Rocky showed his kindness? What are some times that Rocky showed his lack of direction?

Answer 1: Among other things, Rocky likes animals, helps alcoholics move from the street into someplace warmer, will not harm people even though his boss orders him to, encourages street singers, and tries to counsel a neighborhood girl about her reputation. She replies, "Who are you to give advice?" The question is valid. The movie shows us that in spite of his goodness and although he is an athlete, Rocky smokes and drinks after a fight, has been put out of his locker at the gym due to lack of desire, and collects money for a thug as his employment.

Question 2: What is the portrait on the wall of Mickey's gym, where Rocky first trains? What is the caption under the portrait? What does it mean?

Answer 2: The portrait of Christ with the title *Resurrection* is best seen in the first minute of the film, as Rocky enters the gym for the first time. The portrait is symbolic of Rocky's dream and the dream of other fighters—the gym is a place of hope.

Question 3: How does the opportunity to fight Apollo Creed save Rocky's life?

Answer 3: Rocky may not have died if he didn't get the chance to fight Creed, but the chance to fight gave him hope and caused him to make something more of his life. He started getting in shape and training hard to make the most of his opportunity.

Question 4: How does Rocky give these others an opportunity and a measure of hope: Adrian, Mickey, Paulle?

SESSION 1: HOPE

**Give us life, and we will call on your name.
Restore us, O LORD God of hosts;
let your face shine, that we may be saved.**

Psalm 80:18b-19

BACKGROUND

Rocky (1976) is 125 minutes long and is rated PG. It won 3 Academy Awards, including Best Picture.

SYNOPSIS

Second-rate boxer Rocky Balboa is given a shot at the heavyweight title by the flamboyant champ as a publicity stunt. Rocky takes the challenge seriously and dedicates himself to being prepared for the bout. The fight is the climax of the film.

THE POINT OF SESSION 1

The film's message is one of redemption. When Rocky is given a second chance—a sense of hope—he turns his life around. As Christians, we claim Jesus Christ as our Redeemer—the one who gives us a second chance, brings purpose to our lives. We, in turn, are to be a Christ figure for others.

Keep discussion groups large enough so that there is plenty of conversation, but small enough so that everyone feels able to participate. The point of each session should not be read aloud, but kept in mind by the discussion leader while asking the discussion questions and used when absolutely necessary to help the youth understand the purpose.

Answer 4: He accepts the shy Adrian just as she is and demonstrates his care for her, causing her to begin to open up and blossom. He gives Mickey the chance to manage him. He offers Paulle the chance to be a sponsor, giving him some publicity and extra income; he also shows Paulle his love for Paulle's sister, Adrian, whom Paulle had called "a loser."

Question 5: When has someone given you a chance? How did you feel? Have you given anyone a chance? a second chance? Have you ever refused to give someone a chance?

Question 6: While on their date, Adrian asks Rocky, "Why do you fight—because you can't sing and dance?" Rocky responds, "Something like that." Later, Mickey tells Rocky that he has a gift for boxing. What do you think are your special gifts?

Question 7: Rocky loses the "big fight." (A tie is awarded to the champion. Some movie goers have missed that point.) Yet the music is triumphant. Why? Sylvester Stallone, who wrote *Rocky*, didn't know that there would be a *Rocky II*—let alone *III*, *IV*, or *V*. Why did he write a loss for himself in the final scene?

Answer 7: Though oddsmakers say Rocky will not last three rounds, it is Rocky's goal to go the distance—and he succeeds. No one gives him the chance to last, let alone win. If Rocky would have won, some might get the message that nothing matters if you don't win. The message is a realistic one in that it says that victory is found in the trying, that we find redemption if we can hang on to hope.

SESSION 2: FAITH

And the Word became flesh and lived among us, . . . full of grace and truth.

John 1:14

BACKGROUND
Hoosiers (1986) is 115 minutes long and is rated PG.

SYNOPSIS
Hoosiers is based on the true story of Norman Dale, a basketball coach with a hidden past, who shows up in 1951 in Hickory, Indiana, to coach the tiny high school team. His coaching method is questioned and criticized by the townspeople, the acting principal is suspicious of him, and his only supporter is the town drunk. After nearly being run out of town because of a succession of losses, Dale takes the team to the championship of the Indiana State Basketball Tournament.

THE POINT OF SESSION 2
John 1:14 tells us that, "The Word [Jesus] became flesh and lived among us, . . . full of grace and

truth." At first, Coach Norman Dale does not seem to be someone of grace (kindness). His manner is abrasive and his words are direct. He carries a history of assaulting a young player.

As we come to know him, we see a man of strong faith. Coach Dale knows who he is and what he needs to do as a coach to be true to that. He teaches the fundamentals of the game. He does not let others intimidate him out of what he believes to be the right way to coach. He speaks his truth directly to anyone—players, school administration, or townspeople—

who challenges him or stands in his way. In watching him do this, we experience his acts of kindness—his willingness to forgive and give others a chance—just as we experienced similar behavior by Rocky Balboa of *Rocky*.

If we are people of grace, but do not stand up for what we believe to be true, we lack conviction and integrity. If we speak what we hold to be true, but are not kind, we will be harsh, bitter, and angry. *Hoosiers* teaches us to be persons of faith—full of truth and grace.

DISCUSSING & LEARNING

Question 1: The townsfolk say that the coach should play only a zone defense. That is the way it has always been done. What is bad about change? What is good about change?

Answer 1: The female teacher says in a conversation with Norman that a person feels secure, solid, when things don't change. Security and safety are good feelings. On the other hand, new wisdom can be gained and new adventures experienced only when one moves away from the safe and secure center toward the ragged edges of existence. Learning a new method of playing ball is difficult at first, but what are the chances of the team winning the state championship with their old method of doing things?

Question 2: Imagine what happened 20 to 25 years before the story takes place, when Shooter missed his shot at the buzzer and the game was lost. What impact did missing that shot have on Shooter's life? How do you imagine his life might have been different if he had made it? Have you ever had a similar experience in your life?

Answer 2: The first time Norman meets Shooter, Shooter tells him the story of the missed shot. It defines his life. Even his nickname reflects it. His life has been deeply affected by his past failure.

Question 3: What are a few of the events of your life that have made lasting impressions on your self-concept? Have they affected it positively or negatively?

Question 4: Sometimes, Norman Dale seems harsh. He tells an assistant coach that his "coaching days are over," kicks disruptive players off the team, and even loses games to make a point. Yet Norman Dale is the hero of the film. Why is he a hero?

Answer 4: Not because he wins the state championship! Norman Dale's heroic quality is that he stays true to his beliefs and carries out his responsibilities. He was hired to coach the team; and he does what he believes that he must do to accomplish that goal, even if he has to confront some people and lose some games along the way.

Question 5: At one point, Norman says to Shooter's son, "When's the last time anyone gave him [Shooter] a chance?" His son replies, "He doesn't deserve a chance." List places in the film where someone offers another chance.

Answer 5: The principal hires his old friend Norman to coach again after Norman had been banished from coaching at the college level. Norman lets Shooter be an assistant coach and even has himself thrown out of a game to force Shooter to coach. Norman tells Jimmy that he has a gift for basketball but that Jimmy has to decide for himself whether he wants to be on the team, thereby making Jimmy responsible for his own decisions. After the player apologizes, Norman lets the player who had quit back onto the team. Jimmy decides to join the team and forces the townspeople into giving Norman another chance. Shooter's son gives his father another chance and tells him that he loves him.

Question 6: Before the state championship, the minister reads a Bible verse from the story of David and Goliath. Have you ever felt like David—small in the face of a big opponent? What was that opponent? A person? a task? an idea?

Question 7: One of the players often prays before a game. Before the state championship game, the minister prays with the team. What part does prayer play in the arena of sports?

Answer 7: We can't believe that God takes sides. Instead, we must pray that we may do our best in our contests, that we stay focused on the task at hand, and that we are athletes of integrity and honesty. Norman Dale is a success as a coach. He is not redeemed by the state championship, though, but by the path he takes to win it: to be responsible to his duty and faithful to what he believes to be true.

SESSION 3: LOVE

Not that I have already obtained this or have already reached the goal; but I press on to make it my own, because Christ Jesus has made me his own. Beloved, I do not consider that I have made it my own; but this one thing I do: forgetting what lies behind and straining forward to what lies ahead, I press on toward the goal for the prize of the heavenly call of God in Christ Jesus.

Philippians 3:12-14

BACKGROUND

Rudy (1993) is 113 minutes long and is rated PG.

SYNOPSIS

Rudy is based on the true story of Daniel "Rudy" Ruettiger, a scrappy young Irish Catholic who always dreamed of playing football for the Fighting Irish of the University of Notre Dame. After his best friend is killed in a steel mill accident, Rudy decides to pursue his dream. He doesn't let the fact that his grades are poor and that he

is too small and untalented for football stand in his way. The movie depicts his determination to achieve his goal. The result: Rudy plays in the last two plays of an already-won game in his last year of school.

THE POINT OF SESSION 3

Rudy has a love and a passion: Notre Dame football. The film says that sometimes you have to make your own chances. It says that total love and devotion to a task means not being deterred or quitting when confronted by obstacles. It says that some dreams take a long time to come true; but through perseverance and hard work, most dreams can be realized.

DISCUSSING & LEARNING

Question 1: Rudy has a dream of playing Notre Dame football. What do others tell him about his dream? What effect do you think the words of others has on Rudy before he goes to Holy Cross Junior College?

Answer 1: His priest/teacher tells him that "dreamers are not doers." His older brothers tell him that he is too small and uncoordinated. His father tells him the story of his own father's failed farm, saying, "Chasing a stupid dream causes nothing but heartache." (Remember, too, similar opinions from other movies, such as in *Rocky*,

where Rocky says that his father told him, "You don't have much of a mind; you'd better work on your body." And Adrian says that her mother told her just the reverse.) Personal opinion will enter into answering the latter question, but remember that Rudy follows family tradition and works at the steel mill and that he has a girlfriend who wants to get married and settle down before he decides to move to South Bend. He seems to be heading toward the possibility of giving up his dream.

Question 2: What is the event that finally causes Rudy to decide to pursue his dream? What does that character say and do to encourage Rudy?

Answer 2: Rudy's friend Pete is killed in a steel mill explosion. Earlier, Pete had given Rudy a Notre Dame jacket and frequently talked with him about his dream. Also, Pete told Rudy that his father had said, "Having dreams is what makes life tolerable." Such events give Rudy hope. And when Pete is killed, Rudy decides to dedicate himself to living out his hopes.

Question 3: John Wesley, founder of Methodism, once said, "Pray as though everything depends on God; work as if everything depends on you." How does Rudy depend on God and on himself as he pursues his dream?

Answer 3: Rudy can be seen praying, meditating in the chapel, and lighting candles as he keeps preparing himself spiritually for his tasks. He studies, works, and trains hard, participating in extra-curricular activities and looking for any open door that will help him accomplish his goals. He makes his own breaks. (If you can't be on the spirit team, work for the grounds crew!) His determination and attitude are evident as he says over and over, "Have I done all I can?"

Question 4: Have everyone pair up and ask: What is a dream of yours? What are the steps you would have

Question 6: Rudy quits when he doesn't make the dress list for the final home game. What does Fortune, the head groundskeeper, tell him that causes him to rethink his decision?

Answer 6: Fortune tells Rudy that he has already been successful in so much—being on the team and close to receiving a college degree. He tells Rudy that he himself quit the team years before, and it was a decision he has regretted ever since. Rudy sees that his goal of running onto the field just once as a dressed team member may not happen, but there are other victories along the way that matter just as much.

to accomplish to make your dream a reality? What obstacles are standing in your way? Are you still sure that you want to achieve this dream, knowing what has to be done and what obstacles you face? If you are sure, then can you say that you will face up to the challenge and strive to attain your dream? Will you do it?

Question 5: For whom does Rudy say that he wants to play?

Answer 5: Rudy wants to play for everyone who ever had a dream and didn't get to accomplish it, among them his family, Pete, his co-workers at the steel mill, and the like.

CLOSING SESSION

I appeal to you therefore, brothers and sisters, by the mercies of God, to present your bodies as a living sacrifice, holy and acceptable to God, which is your spiritual worship. Do not be conformed to this world, but be transformed by the renewing of your minds, so that you may discern what is the will of God—what is good and acceptable and perfect.

Romans 12:1-2

ACTIVITY 1

Give groups of four to six persons a sheet of newsprint and markers. Have each group create a list of all the qualities of character of a man that they can think of. Also have them write an example of where each quality is depicted in one of the three films watched.

After a few minutes, ask the groups to read aloud their lists. Ask the following questions:
- Does God value these character traits in a man?
- When do society's values differ from God's will?

Make a continuum line on the floor, using masking tape. Identify one end as *10* and the other end as *0*. Using six to ten of the character traits listed by the groups, make statements and ask participants to place themselves on the continuum. For example, for the virtue of honesty, you could say, "With *10* being always, and *0* being never, how often are you willing to stand up for what you believe, even if it means directly opposing others?"

ACTIVITY 2

Read aloud the Scripture for this session—Romans 12:1-2. Give each youth a piece of paper and an envelope. Ask him to write a letter to himself, describing the kind of young man he would like to be in a year. Have each youth include a dream or a goal he'd like to be working toward if he is able. Ask volunteers to read what they wrote. Then have everyone self-address the envelopes and seal the letters within. Collect the letters and plan to mail them to the youth on the first anniversary of the retreat.

CLOSING PRAYER

With the newsprint from Activity 1 visible, have the group stand in a circle. Invite the youth to voice sentence prayers, using the character traits they named earlier. Offer a couple of examples, such as, "God, help me to hold fast to my promises," or "God, I want to be more optimistic in my outlook."

I do not understand my own actions. For I do not do what I want, but I do the very thing I hate.

Romans 7:15

So I will boast all the more gladly of my weaknesses, so that the power of Christ may dwell in me. Therefore I am content with weaknesses, insults, hardships, persecutions, and calamities for the sake of Christ; for whenever I am weak, then I am strong.

2 Corinthians 12:9-10

Am I not free? Am I not an apostle? Have I not seen Jesus our Lord? Are you not my work in the Lord? If I am not an apostle to others, at least I am to you; for you are the seal of my apostleship in the Lord.

1 Corinthians 9:1-2

THE PREACHER FEATURE

One to Five Sessions Based On
The Apostle and *Leap of Faith*

THEME In our weakness, we are made strong; and preachers are as human as anyone else.

PURPOSE Youth will explore the nature of the ministry with regard to who preachers are and how they deal with their own humanity. Youth will also see that God works with us as God finds us, flaws and all, to produce the best possible outcomes for the redemption of creation.

BACKGROUND *The Apostle* (1997) is 133 minutes long and is rated PG-13.

CAUTIONS *The Apostle* is rated PG-13 primarily for a few slips in language, suggestions of adultery, and the lead character's problems with promiscuity. Two scenes involve violence—in one, a man gets hit in the head with a baseball bat.

SYNOPSIS *The Apostle* is a complex tale of a man's struggle to understand himself, his calling, his relationship with God, and his own human failings and weaknesses. After fatally injuring a man, big-time holiness pastor Sonny Dewey (who changes his name to "The Apostle E. F.") seeks to begin a new life by starting a small church in a backwater Louisiana town. His "second chance" is interrupted when his past finally catches up to him, and he willingly takes responsibility for his actions.

VIDEO VIEWING Begin with an opening prayer. Then view *The Apostle* and *Leap of Faith* where recommended in the program. If you've decided to view clips, use the Video Viewing chart below.

Suggestion: *Preview the film on the VCR that you will use with the program. Make note of these key scenes so you can fast forward during the program, using these approximate start-end times and your VCR counter.*

THE APOSTLE

Start Times	Event	Count
Opening	Sonny's first experience with a black holiness preacher	_____
0:03	The accident (Sonny converts a dying man.)	_____
0:13	Sonny preaches.	_____
0:25	Sonny prays.	_____
0:34	Sonny prays about which way to go.	_____
1:03	Sonny preaches on the radio.	_____
1:25	Sonny fights the troublemaker.	_____
1:36	Live radio service, Sonny confronts the bulldozer, and converts the troublemaker.	_____
1:48	The cops arrive for the last sermon.	_____

LEAP OF FAITH

Start-End	Event	Count
0:00–0:07	At the traffic stop: "I know people."	_____
0:30–0:35	Jonas preaches for the first time: "Are you ready for a miracle?"	_____
0:35–0:41	First round of healings	_____
0:48–0:49	Boyd says: "You don't have a church." Jonas replies: "I have a ministry. And if you've ever sat through church, you know that's better."	_____
0:56–1:09	Jonas preaches and answers the sheriff's charges.	_____
1:22–1:29	Boyd's faith heals him.	_____
1:32–1:38	Jonas prays: "Why did you make so many suckers?"	_____

BACKGROUND

Leap of Faith (1992) is 108 minutes long and is rated PG-13.

CAUTIONS

Leap of Faith is rated PG-13 primarily for some profane language and sexual innuendo. Sexual relationships outside marriage are implied.

SYNOPSIS

Leap of Faith is the story of a con man who poses as a tent show evangelist with a healing ministry. His inner struggles to discover who he really is come to a head when a young man is actually healed by faith at one of his services.

MATERIALS

- *The Apostle* and *Leap of Faith* videos (Optional: *Elmer Gantry* video)
- TV and VCR
- Something to write on and with (newsprint pad and markers, chalkboard and chalk, overhead projector and markers)

USING THESE SESSIONS & ACTIVITIES

These sessions and activities could be expanded to fit a number of formats. Because the stories are so complex, it would be best to watch *The Apostle* and/or *Leap of Faith* in their entirety as a group, which would require one full session for each film. Because of this, these sessions might best be used in a short or long retreat format. You should review the video clips with the group even if you have already viewed the whole film together.

BEFORE THE SESSION

Be sure to make preparations for the Learning Activities or games you will be using.

LEARNING ACTIVITY

(This activity is based on the group's seeing either movie or both in their entirety.)

Have the youth make a list (using a large newsprint pad, chalkboard, or overhead projector) of the good things that Sonny (or Jonas) did and the bad things he did.

For instance, Sonny
- fatally injures Horace;
- threatens and intimidates his wife and children;
- is promiscuous;
- tries to seduce Tootsie;
- is often motivated by selfishness.

On the other hand, Sonny
- converts the dying man;
- cares for his mother;
- obviously loves his children;
- preaches sincerely;

- starts the church;
- befriends and cares for Sammy;
- converts the man on the bulldozer;
- feeds the poor;
- takes responsibility for his actions in the end.

Jonas
- admits that he is a con man;
- is almost always motivated by selfishness;
- tricks people into thinking that he knows what is in their hearts;
- preaches without sincerity;
- tries to seduce Marva;
- gets drunk and violent.

On the other hand, Jonas
- obviously loves his friends and takes care of them;
- drives all night to bring Jane a puppy;
- is honest about who he is and what he is doing;
- refuses to take advantage of what happens to Boyd;
- really revives the community's hope and faith.

DISCUSSING & LEARNING

Have volunteers read aloud the Scriptures from Romans and First and Second Corinthians. Then ask the following questions:

Question 1: What makes a good pastor?

Question 2: Can pastors be human and have weaknesses?

Question 3: Do you expect your pastor to have higher standards of ethics and behavior than you do? If so, why is a pastor different from other Christians?

Question 4: Do you have weaknesses? Do you sometimes fail to live up to God's expectations?

Turn to a clean page on the large newsprint pad and talk about the differences between "tent show evangelists" and the pastor of your church. (You might bring in one of

your pastors to supplement this discussion.) Have the youth list the different responsibilities of a local pastor (preacher, teacher, worship leader, counselor, administrator, enabler, visitor, employer, leader, role model, friend, and more).

Question 5: What does your pastor do as part of his or her job that Sonny or Jonas did not do? (Sonny is more like a local pastor than Jonas in that he starts a church and lives out many of these responsibilities at the church he starts.)

Question 6: At one point Boyd points out that Jonas doesn't have a church and Jonas tells Boyd: "I have a ministry; and if you've ever sat through church, you know that's better." What distinction is he making?

Watch or refer to the following scenes in which Sonny or Jonas preaches: in *The Apostle*—Sonny's first experience with a black

holiness preacher, Sonny preaches, Sonny preaches on the radio, the cops arrive for the last sermon; in *Leap of Faith*—Jonas preaches for the first time: "Are you ready for a miracle?" and Jonas preaches and answers the sheriff's charges.

Question 7: How is your pastor's preaching different from these two styles of preaching? (Be prepared to fend off the inevitable "Our pastor's preaching is boring" without being defensive. Emphasize the different styles of preaching.)

Question 8: What do you like about Sonny's preaching? Jonas' preaching? What don't you like about their styles?

Question 9: What do you think makes a good preacher and good preaching?

Question 10: If you could change one thing about preaching at your church, what would that be?

THE APOSTLE PAUL AND THE APOSTLE E. F.

Point out to the youth a few loose parallels between the life of the apostle Paul and the life of the Apostle E.F.:

- First, Sonny hitting Horace with the baseball bat can be seen as roughly equivalent to the stoning of Stephen, which started Paul thinking about his need to be converted (Acts 7:54–8:1).
- Sonny believes that he hears God speak to him in the same way that Paul heard God's voice on the Road to Damascus (Acts 9:1-9).
- Sonny's relationship with Brother Blackwell mirrors the relationship that Paul had with his mentor, Ananias, the man God told in a vision to care for Paul and teach him (Acts 9:10-19).
- And, of course, Paul spent the end of his career in prison, still preaching to anyone who would listen, even to the authorities who held him (Acts 24:24-27).

AFTER THE SESSION

Encourage the youth to show their appreciation to the pastor of your church in a variety of ways. Lead them in a discussion as to how they can personally and as a group show more concern, understanding, and compassion to their pastor.

OTHER DISCUSSION TOPICS

THE NATURE OF CONVERSION

Have someone read aloud Acts 9:1-9 (the conversion of Paul).

In *The Apostle,* watch the scenes in which Sonny fights the troublemaker and Sonny confronts the bulldozer and converts the troublemaker.

Question 1: How does watching the conversion of the troublemaker make you feel?

Question 2: Would you be embarrassed to confront someone this way?

Question 3: Sonny has a confrontational and flamboyant way of connecting with people who need converting. Are there other ways to do this? (nurture, friendship, relationships, inviting persons to be part of a Christian community)

Question 4: God wants us to offer Jesus Christ to others. How can you accomplish that purpose in your life? How have you done it in the past?

"DEATH BED" CONVERSION

Have someone read aloud the parable of the laborers in the vineyard (Matthew 20:1-16).

In *The Apostle,* watch the scene in which Sonny comes upon a traffic accident and converts the dying young man.

Question 1: How does this conversion make you feel?

Question 2: Do you believe that a person should be allowed to wait to the last minute to be saved?

Question 3: What is the problem with waiting to the last minute to be saved? (You might never have the opportunity.)

Question 4: In the parable of the laborers in the vineyard, what does Jesus have to say about waiting to the last minute? (All who come to him receive the same reward regardless of when they come to him.)

HEALING MINISTRIES

Have someone read aloud John 5:1-18 (Jesus heals the man at the pool at Bethzatha).

In *Leap of Faith,* watch the first round of healings and the scene in which Boyd's faith heals him.

Question 1: How do you feel about these kinds of "healing" services?

Question 2: Have you ever been to a healing service or watched one on TV?

Question 3: Does your church have a healing service? If so, how is it different from what you see in *Leap of Faith*?

Question 4: Would you like your church to have some kind of real healing service?

Question 5: What does Jesus have to say about healing in the story we read? (The healing was dependent on the man's act of faith. Jonas didn't heal Boyd; his faith in Jesus is what healed him. Boyd goes to the crucifix, not to Jonas, for healing.)

One of the best resources for discussion on healing is James K. Wagner's *Blessed to Be a Blessing: How to Have an Intentional Healing Ministry in Your Church* (The Upper Room—ISBN: 0-8358-0410-0).

PRAYER

Have someone read aloud Matthew 6:5-14 (Jesus teaches the disciples to pray).

In *The Apostle,* watch the scenes in which 1) Sonny prays and 2) Sonny prays about which way to go. In *Leap of Faith,* watch the scene in which Jonas prays: "Why did you make so many suckers?"

Question 1: How do you feel about the way Sonny prays—shouting at God, being brutally honest?

Question 2: Sonny prays for God to show him which way to turn the car. Do you believe that God wants us to pray about such mundane details? Or was the way Sonny turned the car deeply significant?

Question 3: How do you feel about Jonas' prayer: "Why did you make so many suckers?" (At least he's being honest to himself and God.)

Question 4: How are the ways Sonny and Jonas pray like the ways you pray? How are they different?

Question 5: What does Jesus have to say about prayer when he teaches the disciples to pray? Do Sonny's or Jonas' prayers follow Jesus' teachings?

The Psalms present many opportunities to demonstrate prayers that express anger or frustration with God (for example: Psalms 6, 10, 22, 38, 55, 62, 69, 74, 83, 109, 120, 130, 137, 140, and 143).

WANT YOUR GROUP TO SEE THE "REAL (OR IS THAT *REEL*) DEAL"?

If you want your group to see real tent show healing services that are run by con artists, get a copy of *Marjoe* (1972). Marjoe Gortner was groomed as a child tent show evangelist by his parents when he was only four years old. Later, after he became an adult, he returned to the tent show circuit as a "rock and roll" evangelist. Marjoe began to feel guilty about tricking people and filmed this intriguing documentary that exposes all the "cons" used by the tent show rip-off artists. (Some of these tricks are also used by Jonas Nightengale in *Leap of Faith*.) This film is unique in that no one knew what Marjoe was doing and they trusted him completely. This "total access" to the behind-the-scenes action makes for some of the most chilling documentary footage ever filmed.

ELMER GANTRY

The Learning Activity and many of the Discussing & Learning questions can also be applied to *Elmer Gantry,* which was one of the best films of 1960. Burt Lancaster and Shirley Jones both won an Oscar® for their performances as a tent show evangelist and a prostitute who was once his mistress.

Elmer Gantry is a traveling salesman who, when he preaches as a joke in a bar, discovers that he has a talent to motivate people to give money. Later, he joins the evangelistic road show of Sister Sharon Falconer and helps her move from small towns to the big city. Sister Sharon's tent ministry is nearly destroyed when Gantry meets up with a former mistress at a house of prostitution, which he is forcing the police to close down. When the prostitute clears him of being involved with her in the present, Sister Sharon and Gantry become bigger than ever and open the church that Sister Sharon has worked her whole life to build. When a madman sets fire to the building during a healing service, Sister Sharon refuses to leave and dies in the inferno. Gantry refuses to take her place in the ministry; and when we last see him, he is walking away from the charred remains of the burned-down church with his "followers" crowded around it, singing "I'm on My Way, Up to Canaan Land."

Elmer Gantry was a source for both *The Apostle* and *Leap of Faith,* containing elements and events that you will recognize in the two later films. As a character, Elmer Gantry shares much in common with both Sonny Dewey and Jonas Nightengale. Gantry is a mixture of good motivations and selfish intentions, heroic strength and moral weakness.

MuLan
A Retreat

For we do not proclaim ourselves; we proclaim Jesus Christ as Lord and ourselves as your slaves for Jesus' sake. For it is the God who said, "Let light shine out of darkness," who has shone in our hearts to give the light of the knowledge of the glory of God in the face of Jesus Christ. But we have this treasure in clay jars, so that it may be made clear that this extraordinary power belongs to God and does not come from us.

2 Corinthians 4:5-7

THEME God wants us to discover who we are and what we are called to be through love and grace.

PURPOSE We must learn to love ourselves and see ourselves as unique, individual creations of a loving God. Only then can we learn to love one another unconditionally as Christ loved us.

BACKGROUND *Mulan* (1998) is 88 minutes long and is rated G.

CAUTIONS Mulan dresses as a man to take her father's place in the army. A few remarks are made about cross-dressing; and several of the soldiers go skinny-dipping, but no nudity is shown. Most of the violence is done off screen. The villain is fairly intense by Disney standards, but there is nothing that has not been seen before. As always, be sure to preview the entire movie before showing it to your youth.

SYNOPSIS Pha-Mulan, a young girl, takes the place of her aging, crippled father when her country goes to war. She assumes the identity of a male and trains with the army. When Mulan's army is attacked, it is Mulan's quick intelligence that saves them all. She is injured, and her secret is discovered. She is thrown out and left behind. When the emperor's palace is attacked, it is Mulan who leads her friends in an undercover mission to rescue the emperor. In the end, Mulan is recognized for her bravery. She receives a position of honor in the emperor's staff and returns home to honor her father.

USING THESE SESSIONS & ACTIVITIES

The *Mulan* retreat is designed to be used in three sessions. Each session is preceded by viewing one segment of the movie. Each segment deals with a specific theme. Viewing the entire movie and then discussing it in one session would require a lengthy time slot. Several sessions are recommended if you view this film in a situation other than a retreat format.

MATERIALS

- *Mulan* video
- TV and VCR
- Several large sheets of paper or a roll of butcher's paper
- Markers
- Paper plates
- Scissors
- Pieces of elastic or long rubber bands
- Stapler
- Old newspapers or enough used paper to make lots of paper wads

SESSION 1: THE MASK

THEME We all wear masks of one kind or another. It is important to not let society tell us who we should be but to become who we are in the sight of God.

Begin with a prayer. Then view the first 25:00 minutes of *Mulan,* stopping the tape when Mushu the dragon leaves the village to protect Mulan.

ICEBREAKER

Have the youth form small groups. Hand out the paper plates and ask the youth to draw a mask of themselves as they believe others see them or as they think the world wants them to be. Have scissors on hand to cut out eye holes. Make sure that the youth have their name on the mask somewhere so that the masks can be redistributed later.

DISCUSSING & LEARNING

Take turns talking about how the youth drew their masks.

Ask questions such as these:

Question 1: Is this how the world sees you, or is this how you think the world wants you to be?

Question 2: What does society expect of teenagers today?

Question 3: How do you think that society and its expectations have changed since your parents were teens?

Collect the masks and put them aside. You will get these back out in Session 3, but don't tell the youth.

Question 4: Mulan is painted in a sort of mask so that she will look like all the others. What are Mulan's family's expectations as she prepares to see the matchmaker?

At this point you can bring up lines from the song such as:

"With good fortune and a great hairdo"
or
"With good breeding and a tiny waist"
or
"A sow's ear into a silk purse."

Question 5: In what ways are our society's expectations similar to those of Mulan's village?

In Mulan's song she sings: "Look at me—I am not meant to play this part. If I were myself, I would break my family's heart," and "When will my reflections show who I am inside?"

Have someone read aloud 2 Corinthians 4:5-7.

Question 6: What treasures are inside Mulan?

Question 7: Why do you think the writers had Mulan wipe off half the make-up?

Question 8: Why does Mulan feel like two people? Can you think of a time when you have felt this way?

Question 9: How do we change ourselves in order to fit in?

Question 10: What does it take to be part of the popular group at your school?

Question 11: What other masks do we wear in our lives?

Question 12: What treasures do you have inside that you don't reveal very often?

Remind the youth that the film's tag line is "The flower that blooms in diversity is the most rare and beautiful of all." Mention that Mulan's father refers to the "late blossom."

Have someone read aloud Matthew 13:1-9 (the parable of the sower).

SESSION 2: ROLE REVERSALS

Begin the session with prayer. Then view the second portion of *Mulan* (0:25 to 0:50). Stop the video after the army sings the song "A Girl Worth Fighting For."

PURPOSE The youth will learn about myths about the opposite sex, about how to get along with others, and about perseverance during hard times of trial.

LEARNING ACTIVITY

If possible, clear the room of chairs or move them all to one side of the room. Write the words *True* and *False* on two large sheets of paper. Tape the sheets of paper on the walls that are opposite each other. Have the youth stand in the middle of the room.

Say: "I'm going to read aloud a series of statements. When I say 'Go,' run and stand by the wall that corresponds to how you feel about the statement."

(NOTE: If you are working with a smaller group, this activity works great with a "true couch" and a "false couch." The youth must all be on the couch together. Standing beside it is not allowed.)

While you are playing this game, select individual youth to voice their opinions. Don't allow too much time for discussion of each statement. This game gets bogged down if it doesn't keep moving.

- After all is said and done, it is still basically a man's world.
- The man should be the primary breadwinner in the home.
- The woman is the one better suited to be the child-raiser.

Hang up three sheets of large paper or a large piece of the butcher paper. Write the following three headings at the top: *Birds, Rocky Soil, Good Soil.*

Ask the youth first to talk about where the "birds" are in their lives. Write their answers under the *Birds* heading.

Question 13: What are the things that can kick you back before you can even get started?

Question 14: What are the things that discourage you the most? (You will probably get answers related to parents, school, peers. Write down all these items.)

Then ask the youth about people they know or have heard about who blossomed quickly and then faded away. They may be people the kids know from school. Offer the names of celebrities or groups who seem to have disappeared. Offer suggestions such as young actor River Phoenix or comedian John Belushi, who were at the peak of their careers and then lost it all

because of bad decisions. List these items under *Rocky Soil.*

Finally, ask the youth to name all the things that are "good soil" in their lives. These do not have to be things they already have. They can be things that they believe will make good soil or things that should make good soil.

Question 15: What kind of seed is Mulan? (Point out that Mulan's family prays a lot. The first time we see Mulan's father, he is in prayer. The last thing Mulan does before she runs away is pray.)

Question 16: What are Mulan's motivations to take her father's place?

Say something such as: "Mulan's soil is good. She will grow and be strong and blossom." Then say a prayer for the youth in the group, for their families, and for all the things that make them strong. Pray that God will guide the youth as they grow and become part of the Creator's garden.

- It is the guy's responsibility to ask for the date.
- It is always the guy's responsibility to pay for a date regardless of who asked whom out.
- In the home, cooking and doing the laundry are women's work.
- Housework should be shared equally no matter who makes more money or works more hours.
- Women are the brains of a relationship, and men are the brawn.
- Men suffer from peer pressure more than women do.
- Women put more pressure on themselves than men do.
- Men are naturally better leaders than women are.
- There are no women leaders in the Bible. (Save this as your last question and then pick up the Bible and read Judges 4:4-7.)

DISCUSSING & LEARNING

Mulan cannot understand what it is like to be "a man." The song compares men to "a raging river" yet at night the men go off on their own to pray.

- Ask the guys in your group: "What is the one thing women most misunderstand about men?"

- Ask the girls in your group: "What is the one thing men most misunderstand about women?"

Then ask the whole group:

Question 1: How do men and women approach problem-solving differently?

Question 2: How do men and women approach relationships differently?

Question 3: Do you think that there is any task that men or women are more naturally suited for?

Question 4: Do you think that God had a separate plan for men and women?

Form small groups. Have someone read aloud Philippians 3:12-17.

Question 5: Captain Shang fires an arrow at the top of the pole. He hands the stones to Yao and names them *Strength* and *Discipline.* He says, "You will need both." How does Mulan reach the arrow? Was that cheating?

Question 6: At the beginning of the training, Mulan cannot keep up. She continues to fail but keeps getting up. Being sent home by Captain Shang only fuels her desire to fight harder. How would you apply the verses from Philippians to Mulan's situation?

Question 7: If you were to name two more weights, what would you call them? Remember that they must be used together or they can work against you (possible examples: intelligence and emotion, speed and endurance, creativity and regulation, faith and reason).

Say a prayer, praying for guidance in all friendships. Thank God for all the things that make us different. Ask God to open our minds to the truth and to help us let go of the stereotypes we have come to accept of one another.

SESSION 3: MASK OFF!

PURPOSE Youth will learn about standing up for what they believe in. They will discuss taking off the masks they wear for others and accepting and loving who they are.

DISCUSSING & LEARNING

Return the masks to the youth, and let them attach elastic or rubber bands to them.

View the final segment of *Mulan.*

Ask for volunteers to read aloud the following Scripture passages: 1 Timothy 3:8-16 (leadership), Matthew 12:19-21 (qualities of leadership), Matthew 20:26-28 (leaders must be servants).

Say: "During the battle, it is Mulan who saves her friends. Captain Shang's action would not have saved them. When Shang and his men try to break down the door of the palace, it is Mulan whom they follow. She is a leader. Her gender does not matter."

Question 1: What do the Scriptures say about being a leader?

Question 2: In what way does Mulan possess these qualities that Captain Shang does not?

Question 3: Is it more difficult for a woman to be accepted as a CEO or for a man to be accepted as a nurturing parent?

LEARNING ACTIVITY

Have the youth break into small groups. Hand out the sheets of newspaper or used sheets of paper.

Question 1: Which character is most like you?

Question 2: This is one of the few Disney films in which the villain does not get a song. How many other "villain songs" can you sing? Why do you think *Mulan's* villain does not get a song?

Question 3: When Mulan leaves, we see the eyes on one of the ancestors' statues "blink" and Grandma wakes up, saying: "Mulan is gone." Later we see the ancestor wake up to Grandma's prayer. Is it possible that Grandma can communicate with the ancestors because she is going to be with them soon?

Ask for a volunteer. Have him or her stand in front of the group and put on the mask that he or she created earlier. (Remember this is the mask that represents who others see or who others want the youth to be.)

Have the youth make paper wads and take turns throwing them at the youth in the mask. The masked youth may duck, catch, or hit the paper wads out of the way. Let the throwers start throwing simultaneously. Eventually, the masked person won't be able to keep up with the barrage.

Have the person remove the mask and try again. He or she might get better at defending himself or herself against the barrage.

Gather the group and have volunteers read the following Scriptures: 1 Corinthians 3:10-17 (being tested by fire); 2 Corinthians 5:16-18 (being a new creation).

Say: "Mulan was not an honorable bride. Mulan tried to be a man, but there was no way that she could do that. In the end of the movie, Mulan faces Shan-Yu alone. She is a girl with a sword. It is in this one moment that Mulan becomes who she is. Up until this moment, she was either unsure of herself or trying to please everyone else. It is only when we make the choice to be a child of God that we can become everything God wants us to be."

Gather for a final prayer, saying a prayer such as: "God in heaven, help us take off the masks that keep us from seeing you. Help us take off the masks that hide who we are. Let our faces and our lives reflect your light. Help us to weather the storms of our lives and know that you make us stronger each day. Help us be leaders by first being servants. Help us to be your children. Amen."

GAME: CHANGE

Get a full suit of men's clothing (pants, shoes, shirt, jacket) and a suit of women's clothing (dress, shoes, wig, purse). Place the clothes on two chairs. Divide your group into two teams, guys against girls. Have a relay race.

The first guy must run down; put on the dress, shoes, wig, and purse; and then run to the nearest female counselor and ask: "Does this dress make me look fat?" Then he must return all the items to the chair and tag the next guy in line. The girls must run to the chair; and after dressing, run to the nearest male counselor and punch him in the arm, saying: "How 'bout them Broncos?" (or whatever sports team is popular in your community).

BIBLICAL FORTUNES

Have a full Chinese dinner. A folding table with the legs folded under it is just the right height for sitting on the floor to eat. Stop by a local Chinese restaurant and ask for some chopsticks to use. At the end of the dinner, serve fortune cookies. Prior to the meal, copy the Biblical Fortunes below. Clip out the verses and replace the fortunes in store-bought fortune cookies. This will require some patience. If patience or time is lacking or if fortune cookies are difficult to find, try putting the fortunes into the middle of a sandwich cookie such as an Oreo®.

Too much pride can put you to shame. It is wiser to be humble.—Proverbs 11:2-3 (CEV)	What you gain by doing evil won't help you at all, but being good can save you from death. —Proverbs 10:2 (CEV)
When God is angry, money won't help you.— Proverbs 11:4 (CEV)	Laziness leads to poverty; hard work makes you rich.—Proverbs 10:4 (CEV)
It's stupid to say bad things about your neighbors. If you are sensible, you will keep quiet. —Proverbs 11:12 (CEV)	Hatred stirs up trouble; love overlooks the wrongs that others do.—Proverbs 10:12 (CEV)
If you do your job well, you will work for a ruler and never be a slave.—Proverbs 22:29 (CEV)	If you have good sense, it will show when you speak. But if you are stupid, you will be beaten with a stick.—Proverbs 10:13 (CEV)
Giving an honest answer is a sign of true friendship.—Proverbs 24:26 (CEV)	A kind answer soothes angry feelings, but harsh words stir them up.—Proverbs 15:1 (CEV)
The right word at the right time is like precious gold set in silver.—Proverbs 25:11 (CEV)	It isn't smart to get drunk! Drinking makes a fool of you and leads to fights.—Proverbs 20:1 (CEV)
Good news from far away refreshes like cold water when you are thirsty.—Proverbs 25:25 (CEV)	You may think you have won your case in court, until your opponent speaks.—Proverbs 18:17 (CEV)
The lifestyle of good people is like sunlight at dawn that keeps getting brighter until broad daylight. —Proverbs 4:18 (CEV)	It's stupid and embarrassing to give an answer before you listen.—Proverbs 18:13 (CEV)
Carefully guard your thoughts because they are the source of true life.—Proverbs 4:23 (CEV)	Children who curse their parents will go to the land of darkness long before their time. —Proverbs 20:20 (CEV)

A FANTASTIC RETREAT
A Retreat Based On *Antz* and *A Bug's Life*

Now if you are unwilling to serve the LORD, choose this day whom you will serve, whether the gods your ancestors served in the region beyond the River or the gods of the Amorites in whose land you are living; but as for me and my household, we will serve the LORD.

Joshua 24:15

THEME Whom do we follow and when do we lead?

PURPOSE Youth will learn about being a leader. They will examine what the Bible says are the qualities of leadership and study the lessons of Jesus when he said, "In order to lead you must first be willing to follow." In Session 3 your group will examine how we are all connected and must work together in order for society to function.

CAUTIONS The two movies have similar story lines, but they could not be more different in tone. *A Bug's Life* is bright and cheerful while *Antz* is rather dark and gloomy. *A Bug's Life* contains no objectionable material. *Antz* contains some mild profanity.

BACKGROUND *A Bug's Life* (1998) is 96 minutes long and is rated G. *Antz* (1998) is 82 minutes long and is rated PG.

SYNOPSES

Antz: The central character is an ant named "Z." Z is a worker ant. In Z's world each ant has his or her place in "the colony." The evil General Mandible is plotting an elaborate scheme to wipe out the ants he feels are lesser creatures. Z has fallen in love with Princess Bala. He convinces his friend Weaver, a warrior ant, to trade places with him so he can be near her. Z is the sole survivor of a great battle and unwittingly becomes part of Mandible's scheme. Z "accidentally" kidnaps Princess Bala and both find themselves on a journey in search of the mythical land of "Insectopia." Upon returning to the hill, Z finds out about Mandible's plan and warns the colony. It is only when the ants all work together that they save themselves. Z and Mandible struggle and fall into a deep hole; Mandible is killed, and Z is rescued and becomes a hero.

A Bug's Life: Flik is a worker ant who just wants to "make a difference." In *A Bug's Life,* the ants work most of the season to provide an offering of food for a gang of grasshoppers who have been terrorizing the ants for years. Flik accidentally knocks the offering into the river. The ants must then face the consequences of resupplying the grasshoppers' offering, knowing it will not leave them enough time to gather their own food supply for the winter. Flik sets off on a journey to the city to bring back bigger bugs to defeat the grasshoppers. He returns with a group of circus performers who he believes are great warriors. The ants and the "warriors" work together on a plan to rid the colony of the grasshoppers. It is only when Flik stands up to the gang leader, Hopper, that the colony bands together to defeat its enemies.

HOW TO USE THIS RETREAT

This retreat is divided into three sessions. The first session involves watching the movie *Antz* in its entirety and following up with discussions and activities.

Session 2 requires watching *A Bug's Life* all the way through and then following up with further discussion.

These two sessions should not be done back-to-back. Give the youth time between the sessions.

Session 3 involves comparing various clips and talking about the similar and contrasting messages.

MATERIALS
- *Antz* and *A Bug's Life* videos
- TV and VCR
- Markers
- Large sheets of paper to hang on the walls
- Masking tape
- Balls of yarn (Use one good-sized ball for every ten people.)
- Bibles
- Plastic cups
- Rubber bands
- Construction paper
- Scissors
- String or safety pins
- Various kinds of seeds

BEFORE THE FIRST SESSION

The following is an excellent icebreaker activity that can be done on the first night of the retreat. It gives the teens some insight into those around them as well as getting them in a "buggy" mood.

Put the construction paper, scissors, string, and markers out on a table. Tell the youth you will give them ten minutes to make a nametag. The tag, however, must be in the shape of a bug. The bug they choose should be the one they think is most like them. They must be able to explain why they chose this bug. After everyone has finished, ask each participant to stand and explain what bug he or she chose and why.

Some suggestions:
- Cockroach (They keep coming back.)
- Fire ant (protective of what is theirs, a nasty bite)
- Butterfly (beautiful and elegant)
- Caterpillar (a "someday" butterfly)
- Spider (artistic)
- Bee (a dedicated worker whose results are sweet)

SESSION 1: ANTZ

PURPOSE
Youth will examine the idea of rules—when it is important to follow them and when it is right to break them.

LEARNING ACTIVITIES
View the movie *Antz.*

Post large sheets of paper with the heading "Rules to Follow."

Ask the participants to think of one "rule of life" that they must follow. On the count of three, the youth are to run up to the paper and write down their one rule and return to their seats. Have the adult leaders make a list of some of the items so that they can refer to them during the small-group time. Encourage the youth to come up with as many rules as they can.

Possible categories:
- Stop signs
- Taxes
- Bedtimes
- Curfews
- Family rules
- The Ten Commandments
- Fashion (conformity)
- Dating (respect of boundaries)
- Cheating on schoolwork
- The Golden Rule

[*Author's Note:* At our retreats we have three basic rules for the weekend—Common Courtesy, No Practical Jokes, and If It Ain't Yours Don't Fool With It. If your retreat has similar rules, remind the youth of these at this time. You as a leader can add rules that you feel are appropriate to your group.]

Form small groups. Make sure each group has its own supply of Bibles, markers, plastic cups, and rubber bands.

Have volunteers look up the following verses and be ready to read them aloud when asked:

- Joshua 24:15—Choose whom you will follow.
- Matthew 22:36-37—Jesus tells us the most important rule to follow.
- Luke 5:1-11—Jesus calls the fishermen to follow him.
- John 14:6—"I am the way. . . ."

JUST ANOTHER BRICK IN THE WALL

Question 1: What would it take for you to leave behind everything you have and follow one person? (possible responses: a strong faith, a charismatic leader, the promise of something good at the end)

Question 2: Why do people join cults? (They feel they have nowhere else to turn; they are searching for something to belong to.)

Question 3: In the movie *Antz,* a lot of effort is put forth to make each member of the colony like every other member of the colony. Do you recall any instances where this was evident? (The signs with phrases like "We, Not You" and "Conquer Idleness." In the club, an announcement says "6:15—Time to Dance"; and all the ants get up and dance to the beat of a drum even though there is no music.)

Question 4: Can you think of ways that our society tries to put us in groups and make us the same? (school uniforms, stereotypes on TV, and so on)

Question 5: What are some ways society may view you as a Christian? (a wimp, nice, a Bible thumper, weird, proud of your faith, and so forth)

Question 6: Can you think of ways our church views you as teenagers? (messmakers, troublemakers, slackers, energetic, dependable)

Question 7: How did Z break the rules? (He danced differently and spoke out against everyone's being the same.)

Question 8: How did Jesus break the rules of his day? (He worked on the sabbath, chased the money changers out of the Temple, ate with prostitutes and other outcasts, and so forth.)

Question 9: When we try to be the same as everybody else, we usually succeed. In what ways are you pressured in school to "fit in"? (Dress in the same style of clothes, listen to the same music groups, use the same slang or words.)

Question 10: As Christians, do we put ourselves in a box? If so, how? (We sing the same songs; we do the same kinds of services over and over; we are expected to be nice, not to make noise, not to talk back, to sit up straight, and to do what we're told.)

Question 11: Throughout the movie we see examples of an "order." Breaking the order seems to be unforgivable. Can you think of examples? (Bala visits the workers club, Weaver [warrior] holds hands with Atena [worker], Mandible tries to hide the fact that a worker has tricked them and fought with the warriors.)

Think of some societal rules that are similar in our "colony." (Some people think that people of different races should not date or marry, that the lower class should not associate with the upper class, that cheerleaders don't date computer geeks.)

AND THE WALLS COME A-TUMBLIN' DOWN

Read aloud Luke 5:1-11.

Say something like: Jesus called the fishermen to follow him. Their first response was, "We're not worthy." Sometimes this is how we feel. But Jesus wants us to follow him. He wants us to break out of the molds that "the colony" has put us in and be like him.

Question 1: Can you think of some rules that were broken for the good of a particular society? (Rosa Parks not giving up her bus seat, the people demonstrating in Tiananmen Square, or Christopher Columbus setting out to prove that the world was round.)

Take fifteen plastic cups. As a group, decide on five "foundation rules." Write a few key words on the five cups. Let these be the base of a pyramid. Create each level based on what your group feels are the most important rules, placing the less important rules on higher levels. When the pyramid is complete, let each member of your group take a shot with a rubber band and see how much of the pyramid he or she can bring down.

Question 2: What happens when the bottom (most important) rules are taken out?

Question 3: Ignoring which basic rules in our culture would bring everything down? (The Ten Commandments, respect for all, the Golden Rule)

Question 4: What happens when we break the rules at school? (detention, lower grades, expulsion)

Question 5: Is being part of a colony a bad thing? (It can be if you allow the rules to cloud your judgment.)

Question 6: Is there anything good about Z's colony? (It's comforting to know where you belong; important jobs get done; those not qualified to do a certain task are not forced to do it.)

Read aloud Joshua 24:15.

Question 7: Who made the choices in *Antz?* (Cutter chose not to follow Mandible; Weaver chose to love whomever he pleased; Z chose to follow his heart.)

Question 8: As Christians, we have made the decision to follow God. In what ways can this get us in trouble? (Peers may think we are weird; it makes us outcasts when we don't follow the crowd's behavior, no matter how destructive it is.)

Question 9: Why is it hard to be a follower of God? (It seems like the others are having more fun; it's hard to be good.)

Question 10: What happened to Z when he started to break the rules? (It caused trouble for himself and for others around him.)

Question 11: What happened to the colony when Z took a stand?

Read aloud Matthew 22:36-37.

Question 12: What did Jesus say are the two most important rules? (Love God with all that you are. Treat everyone as you want to be treated.)

Read aloud John 14:6.

Question 13: Jesus did not say, "Follow me, I am the leader." He said, "I am the way." What do you think he meant by this?

Say something like: We have many rules in our society. Some we create ourselves. Many are for our own good; others, we learned, were not. It was only when one person stood up to challenge bad rules that those rules were changed.

One of God's greatest gifts to us is freedom of choice. We can choose which path to follow in our lives, but we have to be willing to live

with the consequences. We can choose not to do our homework, but we have to be willing to receive lower grades. We can choose not to help the homeless or feed the hungry or help those less fortunate than we are, but we have to be willing to live with that choice.

Prayer: God, we want so much to please you. We want to follow your Son's teachings and your word. Help us understand that following you is the right way, though not always the easy way. Help us resist going along with the crowd, even if that crowd is part of the church. Help us follow you even when we must do it alone. Make us your disciples so that we may faithfully follow the greatest leader, your Son, our Lord, Jesus. Amen.

SESSION 2: A BUG'S LIFE

PURPOSE Youth will look at what it takes to be a leader. In *Antz* they talked about choosing whom to follow. In this session they will look at choosing to lead.

WHEREVER HE MAY GO

LEARNING ACTIVITY 1

Play the mirror game. Have the youth pair off and stand facing each other no more than one foot apart. The person with the most recent birthday is the first leader. The other youth is the mirror. The leader begins making a series of motions that the "mirror" must follow exactly. Encourage facial expressions and jumping. After a few minutes switch places and allow the mirror a chance to be the leader.

LEARNING ACTIVITY 2

View the movie *A Bug's Life.*

Form small groups. Have volunteers look up the following Scriptures and be ready to read when asked:

- 2 Chronicles 1:7-13—Solomon prays for guidance to be a good leader.
- Matthew 20:25-28—Jesus talks to the disciples about being a leader.
- Exodus 3:1–4:17—God calls Moses.

RULES OF LEADERSHIP

Question 1: In the opening scene a leaf falls in front of an ant and he

begins to scream, "I'm lost." Why does he think he is lost? (Ants follow the one in front of them; any deviation can cause disorientation.)

Question 2: Is this funny or sad? (Allow for personal opinions.)

Question 3: Can you think of how this works in our culture? (People feel lost when they can't follow the crowd or when changes occur.)

Question 4: Can you think of a specific example? (church members' reactions to changes in the worship service, a parent's reaction to a teen's rearranging his or her room)

Question 5: Hopper, the grasshopper, says "First rule of leadership . . . everything is your fault." What do you think he means by this? Make up five more rules of leadership.

Question 6: What kind of leader is Hopper?

Question 7: What kind of leader is the Queen?

Question 8: What kind of leader is Princess Atta?

Question 9: What kind of leader is Flik?

Read aloud 2 Chronicles 1:7-13.

Question 10: What does Solomon ask for? (knowledge and wisdom)

Question 11: What did he get from God? (wisdom, intelligence, and riches)

Question 12: Why did he get more than he asked for? (because he was unselfish)

Distribute the seeds.

Say: In the film, Flik explains to Dot about the seed—that everything that is in the tree is already right there in the seed.

Question 13: What qualities do you have now that would make you a good leader when you are an adult?

LAST ONE IN IS A . . . LEADER
Read aloud Matthew 20:25-28.

Question 1: If you were "hanging out" with Jesus, wouldn't it be easy to want to be the "greatest"?

Question 2: When you were younger, did you want to have the seat closest to your teacher?

Question 3: Why do people want to hang out with the team when it wins but seem to ignore the team when it is on a losing streak?

Question 4: What was Jesus' answer to James and John? (If you want to be first, you must be willing to be last.)

Question 5: How is Flik like the leader Jesus described? (He tried to help the worker ants, volunteered for a dangerous mission, stood up to Hopper even though he knew he would get pounded.)

Question 6: The bugs from the flea circus were not the greatest performers. When were they at their most effective? (when they put aside their own wants to serve the colony)

ALL SHAPES AND SIZES

Read aloud Exodus 3:1–4:17.

Question 1: How many times did Moses try to get out of God's assignment?

Question 2: If you were Moses and God turned your stick into a snake, would you continue to question?

Say something like: We have a tendency to see Moses in our minds as he appears in the movie *The Ten Commandments* or *The Prince of Egypt.* But even then he tried to get out of the job at least four times. Moses was no different in nature from any of us, but he believed he would have God with him. God has made the same promise to each of us: "I will be with you."

Question 3: Moses did not believe he could be a leader. He didn't believe he could make a difference. How does such a belief keep us from stepping forward? (We're afraid of looking stupid, of being outcasts, of taking responsibility.)

Question 4: What does Jesus say about leadership? (We must be willing to serve.)

Question 5: How did Jesus "lead by serving"? (He healed the sick, ate with outcasts, and washed the disciples' feet.)

Say: Jesus led by being many things.

Write these titles for Jesus (one per line) on a large sheet of paper: Nurturer, Healer, Missionary, Storyteller, Revolutionary, Preacher, Politician, Challenger, Affirmer, Dreamer, Peacemaker.

See if your group can come up with a few more titles to add to the list.

Go around the circle and ask each person to state one way he or she is like Jesus. Others in the group may offer their suggestions as well.

Question 6: Which of these titles or qualities we have named describe the US President?

Question 7: Which of these describe your youth leader?

Question 8: Which of these describe your teachers?

Question 9: Which of these describe Flik?

Question 10: Which of these describe Z?

Question 11: Which of these describe the queens?

Question 12: Which of these describe the princesses?

SESSION 3: GIFTS YOU DON'T NEED TO EXCHANGE

Read aloud Romans 12:4-8.

Show the following video clip from *Antz*, and then the following video clip from *A Bug's Life*:

- *Antz:* approximately 0:59:00—Princess Bala talks with her mother about "her place."
- *A Bug's Life:* approximately 0:50:00—Flik and Atta talk ("I can't do this").

Say something like: We all have a place. God has plans for each of us. Moses did not want to be a leader, but he became one of the greatest leaders in history. Peter did not think he was worthy of following Jesus, yet Jesus called him "the rock on which I will build my church."

Have the youth take turns stating at least one talent they have that God can use. (making friends easily, Bible knowledge, good with children, faith sharing, good listener, athletic, creative, artistic)

Go around the circle again and have the youth state one way they can use the gift they named when they get back to the church.

Again read aloud Romans 12:4-8.

THE WORLD WIDE WEB

View these clips:

- *Antz:* approximately 1:05:00—the escape from the flood. Watch through Mandible's death.
- *A Bug's Life:* approximately 1:20:00—the last battle. Watch through Hopper's death.

LEARNING ACTIVITY

You can do this activity as a large group or in small groups. It is much more effective in a large group, but it is also more challenging.

Have the youth stand side by side in a circle with everyone's shoulders touching. One person holds the end of a ball of yarn and tosses the ball across the circle. That person holds the yarn and tosses the ball to someone else. Have the youth keep a snug hold on the yarn—not tight enough to break it, but enough so that it doesn't droop. One possible rule would be *not* to throw to the person on either side. The idea here is to build a web.

When the last person receives the ball of yarn, he or she is to throw it back to the one who started the web. Clip the end with the scissors and tie the two ends together.

Say something like: We now have a web that connects each person to everyone else. Now, don't let go, but what happens when I do this? (Reach in and pull on one string. Everyone should be affected.)

Next, ask one person to step out of the circle and let go of the yarn. The rest of the group should immediately take up the slack.

Break into your small groups.

DISCUSSING & LEARNING

Question 1: What "webs" are we part of that connect us? (family, friendship groups, sports teams, youth group, church, the body of Christ, the human race)

Question 2: What happened when the youth leader pulled on one string? (Everybody felt the tug.)

Question 3: Imagine that our web is your family. What are some "pulls" that everybody feels? (arguments, fighting, lack of communication, death)

Question 4: Imagine that our web is our youth group. What is a pull that everybody feels? (arguments, the formation of cliques, a group member who stops coming)

Question 5: What happened when one person dropped the string? (Everyone else had to take up the slack.)

Question 6: What happens to a family web when the parents divorce? (The rest must do what they can to keep the web snug.)

Question 7: What happens when one or more persons in the youth group don't keep their end up? (It gets harder to do things, the group feels less close, people start to resent one another.)

Question 8: What happens when more and more people drop out? (The web gets tangled and doesn't resemble a web anymore.)

Question 9: How do we get people to stay in the web, get others back, and bring even more into the web? (Use the leadership skills that God has given us.)

Gather together for a final prayer: God, we thank you for the gifts that you have given us, even if we don't know what they are just yet. And even if we don't know how to use them. We thank you for our gifts just the same. We know that we are connected to one another, to the world, and to you. Help us keep the connections. Help us understand one another when we are hurting. Help us support one another when we are down. Help us make your loving presence known in our world by being your leaders and following your son Jesus. Amen.

A DEVOTIONAL FOR YOUTHWORKERS:
A Bug's Life

Dear Youthworker,

If you watched *A Bug's Life,* when the queen started talking about "this is the way we've done it since I was a pupa," you cringed, didn't you? Many of us immediately identified with Flik. He's a young guy. He has ideals. He comes up with these really "out there" ideas, and what happens? No one will give him a chance. All he wants to do is make a difference.

Sound familiar?

It has been said that the seven last words of the church will be, "We've never done it that way before."

In addition to the queen's words, there were other lines that probably rang a bell:

"Everybody is just waiting for you to screw up."
"We've always done it this way."
(and my personal favorite:)
"It's not our tradition to do things differently."

You've probably read that the average tenure of a youthworker is about eighteen months. We show up. We have new and wonderful ideas. Kids like us. We just want to make a difference.

Then reality sets in.

"You did *what* in the youth room?"
"The kids put a stain on the Miriam Fassbinder memorial wood paneling again?!"
"It is not our tradition to do things differently."

It's easy to feel like Flik. It happens to all of us.

"Not that I am referring to being in need; for I have learned to be content with whatever I have. I know what it is to have little, and I know what it is to have plenty. In any and all circumstances I have learned the secret of being well-fed and of going hungry, of having plenty and of being in need" (Philippians 4:11-12).

"So let us not grow weary in doing what is right, for we will reap at harvest time, if we do not give up" (Galatians 6:9).

Paul wrote the Book of Philippians while chained to another human being, yet he talks about having learned to be content. In Galatians he said not to lose heart in doing good for God.

Isn't that what we're about as youthworkers? We are doing good for God and then a swarm of grasshoppers lands on us with both feet (they come, they eat, they leave; they come, they eat, they leave; they come, they eat, they leave).

Jesus did not say, "I come so that all things can be, uh . . . pretty much the same as they always have been." Jesus said, "I come so that all things can be made new."

"We know that all things work together for good for those who love God, who are called according to his purpose" (Romans 8:28).

It's easy to feel down when the grasshoppers are after us, but it's harder to deal with when criticism comes from our own team. But God does cause all things to work together.

You know that's true. You know you can name specific instances when you thought everything was going wrong, and something wonderful came out of it.

Be strong. Be filled with the Spirit. Let the love of God move through you. Remember that if Jesus Christ himself couldn't please everybody, why should you think that you can?

> Pray this prayer:
>
> God, sometimes we wonder if you are there.
>
> We want so badly to please you, God. We want so much to share your love with those we've been entrusted to teach. But sometimes it gets so hard. Be with us, God. Be in our hearts so that we may never fear those who speak against us. Be with us so that change doesn't hurt so much. We know you are with us always.
>
> Help us to open ourselves to your presence in our lives.
>
> Amen.

THE FINE PRINT

Q Motion pictures are protected by federal copyright laws. Do these copyright laws apply to showing movies in our church youth group?

A Yes. Under the law, for-profit and nonprofit organizations are required to have a public performance license to show movies, which include purchased and rental videocassettes.

Q How does my church obtain rights to show full-length films and film clips for youth group and other Christian education purposes?

A You need to obtain a public performance license (sometimes called a site or umbrella license) to show movies on home video publicly, even for educational purposes. An umbrella license can be granted by The Motion Picture Licensing Corporation. The MPLC's Church Desk handles these requests. Contact Harald Bauer, Executive Vice President, at 800-515-8855 (fax 203-270-8830).

Q What is an umbrella license and what does it allow the church to do?

A An umbrella license is a 12-month license purchased by your church that enables you to use copyrighted films of your choice for preaching and teaching. If your church purchases an umbrella license, you may use entire videos or clips not only in your youth group with WEEKEND AT THE MOVIES, but your pastor may also use clips with sermons.

Q How much will an umbrella license cost?

A Generally, the umbrella license costs $95 for a 12-month period.

Q Are there any less expensive alternatives?

A Yes. Many denominations—through conferences, jurisdictions, dioceses, and other structures—already have public performance license agreements for their churches. Under these agreements, the church office negotiates with the MPLC a much lower rate per church. If your church's jurisdiction has an umbrella license for its churches, your church can qualify for the lower rate. If you're not sure, call your church's jurisdictional offices and ask whether an umbrella license agreement exists or is being pursued.

Q Without an umbrella license, are there ways to incorporate current film and WEEKEND AT THE MOVIES in our youth group study?

A If a featured movie, though no longer current, happens to be playing at the "dollar theater," your group can pay admission price, see the movie during an outing, and discuss the WEEKEND AT THE MOVIES session afterward or during another group time.

Q Are there other restrictions, even if we purchase an umbrella license?

A Yes. You may use only pre-recorded videos, such as those purchased legally by an individual or rented from video stores or the public library.

You may not dub selected clips on another cassette to show to your group—the clip must be cued from the original pre-recorded tape. No license exists for showing movies taped from television or cable.

If you have any questions about your legal rights, call The Motion Picture Licensing Corporation at 800-515-8855.

THE COPYRIGHT LAW

- The Copyright Act grants to the copyright owner the exclusive right, among others, "to perform the copyrighted work publicly" (Section 106).

- The rental or purchase of a home videocassette does not carry with it the right "to perform the copyrighted work publicly" (Section 202).

- Home videocassettes may be shown, without a license, in the home to "a normal circle of family and its social acquaintances" (Section 101) because such showings are not "public."

- Home videocassettes may also be shown, without a license, in certain narrowly defined "face-to-face teaching activities" (Section 110.1) because the law makes a specific, limited exception for such showing. *There are no other exceptions.*

- All other showings of home videocassettes are illegal unless they have been authorized by license. Even "performances in 'semipublic' places such as clubs, lodges, factories, summer camps, and schools are 'public performances' subject to copyright control" (Senate Report No. 94-473, page 60; House Report No. 94-1476, page 64).

- Institutions, organizations, companies, or individuals wishing to engage in non-home showings of home videocassettes must secure licenses to do so—regardless of whether an admission or other fee is charged (Section 501). This legal requirement applies equally to profit-making organizations and nonprofit institutions (Senate Report No. 94-473, page 59; House Report No. 94-1476, page 62).